Kamakwie

Kamakwie

FINDING PEACE, LOVE, AND
INJUSTICE IN SIERRA LEONE

Kathleen Martin

Red Deer PRESS

For Kieran, Daddy, and Rosie, encircled here

Published by Red Deer Press, A Fitzhenry & Whiteside Company
195 Allstate Parkway, Markham, ON L3R 4T8
www.reddeerpress.com

Published in the United States by Red Deer Press, A Fitzhenry & Whiteside Company
311 Washington Street, Brighton, Massachusetts, 02135

Edited by Peter Carver
Cover and text design by Blair Kerrigan/Glyphics
Photographs by Kathleen Martin except as follows:
6 by Stachoo; 22, 42, 146, 162 by Heather Logan; 49, 92 by Janet Roth; 126 by Nathan Wickett
Photo of Kathleen Martin by Sandor Fizli/Progress Magazine
Printed and bound in Hong Kong , China by Sheck Wah Tong in September 2011, job #56605

5 4 3 2 1

We acknowledge with thanks the Canada Council for the Arts, and the Ontario Arts Council for their support of our publishing program. We acknowledge the financial support of the Government of Canada through the Canada Book Fund (CBF) for our publishing activities.

 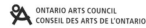

Library and Archives Canada Cataloguing in Publication
Martin, Kathleen, 1973 -
    Kamakwie: finding peace, love, and injustice in Sierra Leone / Kathleen Martin.
ISBN 978-0-88995-472-4
    I. Kamakwie (Sierra Leone)--Social conditions--21st century. 2. Kamakwie (Sierra Leone)--Biography. I. Title.
DT516.827.M37   2011 966.405   C2011-905138-9

Publisher Cataloging-in-Publication Data (U.S)
Martin, Kathleen.
    Kamakwie : finding peace, love, and injustice in Sierra Leone / Kathleen Martin.
[176] p. : col. photos. ; cm.
    Summary: A chronicle of several weeks spent in the tiny village of Kamakwie, Sierra Leone, speaking to the people about their lives, their aspirations, and their memories of war.
ISBN: 978-0-88995-472-4 (pbk.)
    1. Sierra Leone – Social conditions – 1961 – Juvenile literature. 2. Sierra Leone -- History -- Civil War, 1991-2002-- Personal narratives – Juvenile literature. 3. Child soldiers – Sierra Leone – Interviews – Juvenile literature. I. Title.
966.404 dc22   DT516.827.M36785   2011

CONTENTS

PROLOGUE

I had been waiting for Mama J's email. She went back to Sierra Leone a few months after we had been there together. I only spent three weeks in the town of Kamakwie, but I missed it — the people mainly. But also the stories, the music, the dancing, the fried plantain chips, the granat stew. And I missed how much easier it was in Sierra Leone to really see things — as though you were shooting pictures with a telephoto lens, background distractions blurred away.

I had just settled down at my desk the morning the email came. I couldn't open it fast enough.

Hey girl! it began. Cheery. Like Mama J.

Our trip was so good but so short. We had little time in Kamakwie, which was sad, but you know we got a lot done, and at least I got there. The kids came running into my arms, and it was sooo sweet.

I could see the smiles as though the kids were in front of me — Brimah, White Boy, Abu, Binty, Maria, Isotu. I could see the slant of their bodies and hear the crunching stones on the hard dirt as they ran fast around the corner of the bunkhouse to meet the white World Hope truck.

We spent some time in Kakissy. I had the kids there chanting "community!" I would stop them if they started with another topic, and get them back to "community."

My ears still held the memory of the sound of the crowd of Kakissy kids happily yelling out the names of the teams I'd made up. An image of the little boy in the orange shirt jumping in the front row flashed in my mind — then the kind eyes of the Kakissy village chief.

Mama J's email continued, *I do have sad news. Marie died.*

The words on the screen stopped making sense to me.

Marie! Marie! Her name filled my mind. *No! Please, no.*

I wished that I could unread that sentence. I wished that I hadn't opened the email. I sat very still in my chair. Breathing. Useless.

Nurse Adama says the father got upset with Marie being in hospital for so long, so he took her out, wrote Mama J.

My eyes searched down the screen. Marie's father was certain her sickness was witchcraft. He carried her home to their village. She died. Adama visited Marie's grandmother to offer condolences.

Of course she died, I thought when I could think again. *Of course. My sweet starving girl.*

Lots of children die in Sierra Leone. It's easy to find the numbers if you look. Some years, more children under the age of five die in Sierra Leone than anywhere else in the world.

But Marie was eight. Still not safe.

When I went to Sierra Leone, I knew I would meet people who were hungry and who were sick. I knew to expect houses that were small and that didn't have bathrooms. I knew I would see things that would make me sad.

And I knew, from a trip I had taken before to an achingly poor part of India, that I would also find happiness growing like determined wildflowers — seemingly oblivious to the troubles around.

But there was so much I did not know. I did not know the vast darkness of war. I did not know how vicious fate could be. I did not expect at times to feel as if I were imprisoned in a dream where, no matter how I shouted or waved my arms, I could not be heard or seen.

I am a white North American. I grew up in both Canada and the United States. I cannot tell you what it is like to live in Sierra Leone. I cannot pretend to know the minds of the people I met and loved in that country. But I can tell you about what it was like for me to be there. I want to show you the pieces of that experience.

It is important for me to do this because Marie was not disposable. She had a heart and a brain, just like me. She looked at the same moon and knew the same feeling of warm sun on her back. It is not okay that she starved to death. It is not acceptable.

It is important for me to do this because in that dreamlike state, the people I met in Sierra Leone were shouting and waving, too. It was the North Americans — my people — who couldn't hear us, who couldn't see us.

But maybe you could try.

"You were Real to the Boy," the Fairy said, "because he loved you. Now you shall be Real to everyone."

— Margery Williams, *The Velveteen Rabbit*

ARRIVAL

The streets of Freetown are dark. The World Hope truck jolts slowly away from the ferry dock. I am worried. It has to be close to 2 AM, yet there are people everywhere, crossing in front of us. There are no sidewalks. There seems to be no order. The line of cars is tight. What if we hit someone? People are close up against the side of the truck. Our white faces are conspicuous.

Avoid large crowds. Maintain security awareness at all times, the Web site of the United States Department of State had advised. I read its information on traveling to Sierra Leone in the weeks before I left.

Lungi Airport is located across a large body of water from Freetown. The ferry terminal is located in East Freetown, which has a higher crime rate than other parts of the capital. Law enforcement authorities usually respond to crimes slowly, if at all.

The warnings cycle through my mind as though I'd memorized them.

They are interrupted when my son Aidan's voice floats into my head. He is just four, and he held my hand through dinner last night before my flight left.

"I will look right at the moon, Mama," he said. "I will find it in the sky." His eyes, brown like liquid chocolate, were scared. I promised him that if he were lonely for me, looking at the moon would help.

"I will be looking at the same moon in Sierra Leone, and thinking of you," I said, trying to be cheery. "The same moon. It will connect us. I'm not gone long, sweetie. You'll be just fine."

Kate, my two-year-old daughter, was sure I wouldn't leave her behind in Canada. "Mama," she said as I got out of the car at the airport, "we will sit in the back of the plane. Mama and Kate together. Aidan will sit with Dad in the front."

Why did I leave them to come here? What am I doing in this place, in this truck, with people I met for the first time on the plane? The Department of State Web site classifies Sierra Leone as "recovering" from a ten-year civil war, and then lists pages and pages of things to worry about when you get here.

"Steven," I say. Steven is our driver. He does not turn around.

"Hello, Steven. Steven?" I lean closer to the front seats.

"Yes." He is concentrating on the road. Our headlights shine dimly.

"Steven, are there no streetlights in Freetown?"

"Yes, there are streetlights. Look here." He points up. Through the darkness I can see the shape of streetlights and poles along some parts of the road.

"Oh. I see. But they are turned off. Steven, why are they turned off? It makes it so hard to see."

"They have been turned off because of the war. There is no power. They worked before the war."

"They haven't turned them back on again yet? No way!" This is from Nathan, who is sitting next to Steven. I can see his eyebrows raised in surprise above the thin metal frames of his glasses. This is Nathan's first trip to Sierra Leone, too. "But the war ended, like, five years ago, didn't it?"

"Yes, in January of 2002. Six years next month."

"Well, when are they going to turn the lights on again?"

"I am unsure of that."

Steven's answers are short, but not unfriendly. It feels like he's saying as little as possible. It's awkward for him, I suppose. His boss, Brimah Samura, is in the truck behind us. It took two vehicles to fit everyone with their luggage. Maybe Steven is worried he'll say something wrong and get in trouble. Or maybe he's just watching the road.

Multi-vehicle accidents are common, the State Department voice in my head reminds me. *The chance of being in an accident increases greatly when traveling at night.*

I settle back into my seat, staring hard out the window, praying we'll make it safely to the hotel. We are moving more quickly now. I can see the outlines of low buildings crowding the edges of the street.

"There," Steven says after a few minutes. "Can you see there? That is the cotton tree."

I sit up as we pass by the massive, muscular trunk. The branches disappear into the night sky.

"The people who came and had the thanksgiving service under that tree, the freed slaves, they were from Nova Scotia," I say.

"Yes, the Nova Scotians," says Steven.

"That's where I live now," I say. "That's where my home is. I've come from Nova Scotia."

"From Nova Scotia?! Ah!" Steven looks into the rearview mirror briefly, smiles and nods his head.

I think of my friend Joanne, who lived in Freetown for a few years long before the war. She loved that our province was connected to Sierra Leone.

"Sierra Leone was a very friendly country," she had said, handing me a cup of tea. We were sitting at her dining table, the late October light coming in through the back window. "They were like Cape Bretoners or Newfoundlanders. The nicest people you'll ever meet." I reached for the sugar, and she stopped talking for a few seconds.

"I can only assume they continue to be that way, even after all they've been through." She paused again, and looked me right in the eye. "Kathleen, that war wasn't like them. Not at all."

Steven swings the truck up a hill.

I keep looking through my window at the sky, searching for a bit of moon amidst the clouds.

Selling charcoal in Freetown

FREETOWN

In Freetown, every type of thing is for sale: lemons, shoes, antennas, luggage, towels, eggs, bananas, jewelry, small bags of water. I see someone with a mattress and someone else with long pieces of rebar. People walk along the side of the road with the things they are selling balanced on their head. I am most amazed by the women who carry charcoal in round woven baskets stacked as many as eight high. The weight must be incredible.

"You North Americans carry your loads on your back," Brimah Samura says, pointing to my blue backpack. "In Sierra Leone, we carry them on our heads. Before you leave, we will teach you. You can do it at home, then." He laughs heartily, the corners of his eyes crinkling.

Brimah Samura is the director of the Kamakwie Wesleyan Hospital, and is our guide in Freetown. Kamakwie, our final destination, is a day's drive away — what Brimah Samura calls "up-country." Today we are on our way to the World Hope Sierra Leone office to meet its director, Saidu Kanu, and to discuss our plans for Kamakwie. We pass buildings painted in cheerful colors: yellow, pink, blue, orange. Some have striped shutters thrown wide open. All have roofs, and sometimes walls, that are patchworks of rusting corrugated metal.

There are five of us going to the office with Brimah Samura. Heather, Janet, Jennifer, and Nathan are a medical team come to help at the hospital. Heather and Janet have been to Sierra Leone twice before together as volunteers for World Hope Canada, the charity that supports the hospital. Heather is a doctor and Janet is a nurse. Jennifer and Nathan work with Heather at the hospital in Fredericton, New Brunswick, where they live. Jennifer is a doctor, finishing the last part of her residency, and Nathan is an emergency-room nurse.

The World Hope office is on the top floor. The stairwell is hot, despite the windows at the landings. About thirty women in bright-patterned dresses line one wall on our way up. We squeeze past them. Finally, Brimah Samura leads us into an open room with a large table in the center.

"What are the women waiting for?" I ask him.

A side street in Freetown

"They are here about small business loans," says a man, who is quickly crossing the room to shake hands with Brimah Samura. "We are the largest microcredit lender in Sierra Leone. I am Saidu Kanu." He reaches out his hand to me. "Welcome to Freetown!"

Saidu Kanu is slender and carefully dressed. He moves with assurance, his deep-set eyes swiftly assessing our group. He breaks into a smile. "Dr. Heather! Nurse Janet!"

"Saidu Kanu! Brother! It's good to see you!" says Heather. She shakes his hand enthusiastically.

"You are back again! How many times is this?"

"Third trip," says Janet.

"Praise God!" says Saidu Kanu. "Come back into my office."

We squeeze onto chairs in the small room. Brimah Samura stands, his large frame blocking the doorway. He leans an elbow on the filing cabinet.

"So, tell me your plans," says Saidu Kanu, leaning back in his chair. "First, who is going to be the leader of this group? Is it you, Dr. Heather? You need a leader."

"Okay," says Heather, glancing at Janet. She pushes her long brown hair back from her face. I can see her cheeks flush. "Okay," she says again, this time more formally. "First, let me introduce you to Dr. Jennifer, who is my student at the hospital where I work in Canada. She is going to be doing presentations in the villages around Kamakwie about keeping babies and young children healthy. We did research when we were here last to see the kinds of information that would be most important. Dr. Jennifer has created posters that show pictures of the information, too. We will leave these at the hospital when we go so the nurses can use them."

Saidu Kanu nods. "Good." He is paying close attention, but I can see he is thinking — balancing what Heather says against the list of needs he must hold in his head.

"Nathan is a nurse, and he will help us with the presentations. And you know Janet."

"I'll be following up on my Alpha kids," says Janet. "I want to see how they're doing at home."

"Yes, good. And Dr. Heather, you will spend some time working in the hospital, too?"

"My plan is to be in the villages mostly," says Heather. "We need to try and prevent people from becoming sick in the first place. We want to keep them from having to go to the hospital."

"I see. Yes. But you will have some time in the hospital, I hope."

Heather says nothing. Saidu Kanu turns to me. "And you are the writer."

"Yes," I say. "World Hope Canada asked me to come here to research health issues facing young children for a book."

"You will be with this team, but independent of this team," says Saidu Kanu.

"I suppose so. Yes."

"We will try and show you everything you might need to see."

"Thank you."

"We will help with whatever you need. It is important that people know what is happening here." Saidu Kanu speaks directly to me. He is not smiling. I notice the deep line between his eyes. "It is very important. We worry, now that the war has been over for a few years, that people from other parts of the world will stop being interested in Sierra Leone."

I'm not sure what to say. I begin to feel slightly anxious. He is so serious. "We still need help."

"Yes." I wish he would look at someone else. Back at Heather.

Saidu Kanu smiles brightly. "Okay, now we must change your money from American dollars to leones. Nurse Janet, you shall be in charge of the team's money. You look like you will be good at that. It is about three thousand leones to the dollar."

While Janet and Heather, Brimah Samura and Saidu Kanu painstakingly count and sign off on stacks of leones, I walk back into the large room, over to one of the windows. Two teenage girls walk along the street below, wearing their school uniform — a purple gingham dress with sharp box pleats at each hip and a belt at the waist. The girls look crisp against the dusty road.

After they pass, I notice three children looking up at me from across the street. I wave. They wave back. They keep staring and smiling. My camera is slung across my chest. I take it out of its case, and snap a photograph of them. Then I use the zoom on my lens to bring them closer so I can have a better look. Two boys and a girl are standing next to a tall stool that holds a plate piled with nuts. One boy is wearing bright orange shorts, torn at the knee; the girl's shirt is trimmed in lace. I snap another photo. Nathan and Jennifer come and stand next to me and begin waving, too.

When we finally walk down to the street, I get a closer look at the kids. They are standing under a long green sign on which someone had painted *Momoh's Carpentry Workshop* in red capital letters. The kids continue to smile and wave at me.

The kids at Momoh's Carpentry Workshop

The older boy, who must be about seven, puts his arms around the two younger ones. I take another photograph, and then notice another older boy standing off at the corner of the building. He has a big blue-and-brown tub full of plastic dishes on his head.

They aren't in school, I realize. *They should be in uniforms — the older ones, certainly. They should be in school.*

I lift my camera again. A little girl in a pink satin dress with a frilly heart pocket runs from behind a cooler that is balanced on a bench. She jumps in front of the others, happily flinging her arms wide. Just as I take the photograph, the girl with the lace on her shirt holds out her hand.

"She wants to be paid," Janet says, as she comes up to me. "You can't just go taking pictures on the street. You can up-country, but not in Freetown. I got in trouble from the police for taking a photograph of the cotton tree last time I was here. They wanted to take my film."

"Oh, God. I don't have leones yet. I can't pay her," I say. "Where's Brimah Samura?"

"He's finishing up with Saidu Kanu. He'll be down in a minute. Don't worry about it this time."

I look over at the kids and try smiling at them. I put my camera away, feeling awful. Then I turn my back to them. Heather is waiting for me.

"What are you going to do here?" she asks. She sounds annoyed. I haven't decided whether or not I like her. I certainly don't have to answer to her.

"I beg your pardon?"

"What are you going to do here?"

"I'm researching a book, Heather. You know that. I'm going to talk to people to learn as much as I can about the issues kids here face."

"So they're going to give you information."

"Yes." I am getting irritated.

"That's what the people in Kamakwie are going to do for you. What are *you* going to do for them?"

Nathan and Jennifer were staring at the ground while Heather spoke. Now they look at me. Janet is beside me.

"We're going to a hospital, Heather. I'm not a doctor. I have no medical training."

She does not shift her gaze. She waits.

"Umm . . . can we go to a school? I brought picture books with me. I could read them at a school. Or, I could . . . " I am trying to think. I was not expecting this. "I could do a writing workshop. I do those at schools all the time. I could help them write a newsletter. Maybe something to do with health. Could we get paper here? They probably don't have a lot of extra paper at the schools. I could bring paper and hold the workshop."

I can see Brimah Samura coming out the door toward us.

Heather grins instantly. "Awesome! Awesome idea! Let's do it! Can we help, too? It'll be so much fun! We haven't done something like that before. Brimah Samura, brother!" she calls. "We need to buy some paper!"

I turn toward the street again, relieved. The children at Momoh's workshop stretch their palms out toward me, smiling hard. I notice adults behind them now, leaning against the building's bright blue wall. I shake my head. "I'm sorry," I call. "I'm sorry."

Janet puts her arm around my shoulders as we walk away.

Steven, our driver, in the white World Hope truck

MINISTRIES

MOVING UP-COUNTRY

"Don't wear white," Janet warns me as we get dressed the day we're driving to Kamakwie. We are roommates. "You should never wear white on travel days."

"Why?"

"You'll be brown with dust by the time we get to Kamakwie."

Janet loves West Africa and visits every time she can pull enough money together. She usually goes to Sierra Leone or Ghana.

"I have pictures of all of the kids I sponsor on a table at home," she said to me the first night. "My sons laugh when they show their friends. They say some mothers collect things like spoons, and I collect sponsor kids."

It's easy to tell Janet is a mom. Her three boys are grown, but she is still in mode, managing details. Like not wearing white. Like remembering to fill the wash bucket at the hotel with water.

"The toilets always break," she explains. "This way you can still flush."

She carries a giant woven brown purse everywhere that reminds me of Mary Poppins's carpetbag. It seems to have anything you might need: hand sanitizer, sunscreen, a camera, snacks, paper, an extra bottle of water.

Janet has been itching to get to Kamakwie since we arrived. She wanted to go up-country right away, but Heather insisted that we spend a few days in Freetown so Jennifer, Nathan, and I could see it. Steven drove us around, to see the cotton tree in the light, to shop at the Freetown market, to swim at Lumley Beach.

"Things are different in Kamakwie," says Janet as I slip my camera strap over my shoulder on our way out of the hotel room. She had seen me trying to shoot photos surreptitiously through the open truck window as we explored Freetown. "You can take as many photos as you want."

Heather and Janet hop into Brimah Samura's truck. Jennifer, Nathan, and I climb in with Steven. I sit in the front. Steven is a little more relaxed now. He still waits to speak until he is spoken to, but he will give longer answers. There have been a few times when he has forgotten himself, and laughed really hard. Yesterday we were trying to get him to teach us how to speak in Krio. We all had *kushe* down, which means "hello."

"How do you say something else?" Nathan asked.

"What else?" Steven looked at us, blocking the sun from his eyes with his hand. "What kind of thing do you want to say?"

"How about 'How are you?'"

"*How de body*."

"How-dee-bah-dee?"

"Yes." Steven smiled.

We all practiced.

"Like 'how's your body?'" I said.

"What?"

"It sounds like 'how is your body.' How-dee-bah-dee," I said it again, more quickly. "Hey, Jennifer! How-dee-bah-dee?"

Steven was trying not to laugh.

"How do you spell it?" I asked. "Wait. I'll just write it out like it sounds. Okay, Steven. Pretend that we just met you. See if we can pass for Krio speakers."

"All you white people?" Then he shook his head and laughed and laughed.

It was nice to see. Steven usually has such a concerned expression. I can't tell how old he is. Thirty? Forty? But when he laughs, he seems younger. The lines on his forehead disappear.

We drive slowly through the Freetown traffic. I snap pictures of the side streets falling from the main road. Deep crevices cut through them like veins. People have to jump over them. Even though it is mid-morning, young people are everywhere, sometimes talking in groups, but a lot of the time just watching — I'm not sure what.

As we leave the city, the road is lined with tall grasses. Every now and then there is a house, sometimes made of concrete blocks, sometimes of clay bricks. When there are children by the side of the road, we wave at them.

One little girl is wearing a dark blue dress with a white collar. It is too big for her, and sits half off one shoulder. I can see her starting to run across the yard as the truck approaches. The other kids she is with are older. They walk. She is well ahead of them. She stops and turns triumphantly toward us. Then she screams. Again and again and again. I can see her little round mouth open wide, her body shaking, her eyes terror-stricken. The bigger kids come running.

"Oh my God," says Jennifer. "Oh my God, what's wrong?"

"Should we stop?" I ask.

"They are not used to seeing white people," says Steven, glancing at the child as she disappears in his rearview mirror. "She thinks you are a ghost."

"Oh, no!" says Jennifer, looking behind us down the road. "She was really scared."

We are quiet.

"I suppose if you're used to seeing people with dark skin, it would be kind of freaky to see us," says Nathan.

"Totally," I say.

"It's you, Jenn," Nathan teases. "Your hair isn't even brown. It's your blonde hair that put her over."

Maybe she thinks we're bad luck. Maybe she'll have nightmares now. Ghosts come to life. How awful to be someone's nightmare.

It is hot in the truck, even with the windows open. I put the lens cap on my camera and tuck it next to me on the seat, covering it with the edge of my skirt to keep it out of the dust and the sun.

The upper hospital grounds. Our bunkhouse is on the
right. You can just see the edge of the porch — the dark
line jutting off the right-hand side of the building.

KAMAKWIE

O ur bunkhouse is turned away from the paths of red-brown dirt that split like the points of a star through the hospital grounds. The kids have to walk all the way around the building, across scrub grass, to get to our front porch. The porch is wide and set high off the ground like a stage. It is empty, except for a long blue wooden bench.

In the morning, I stand on it and watch the sun smudging its way through the darkness, shifting the December sky from gray to blue. Pa Brimah is there, sitting in front of the corrugated metal goat shed just at the edge of our yard. The black-and-white goats bury their triangle faces in the field behind him. Pa Brimah keeps watch for us. I'm not entirely sure what that means, other than that he is always at his perch near the bunkhouse. I can't picture Pa Brimah, with his constant toothy smile and fuzzy goatee, scaring anyone away. But you never know, I suppose.

The kids had come running to the porch last night when we arrived. Another Brimah was first. He looked to be about ten.

"Brimah!" Heather cried, a giant smile on her face. She did not run over to him, like Janet did, arms wide, calling out "My Brimah! My Brimah!" Heather held back for a minute, just drinking him in. I watched her eyes, love streaming out of them.

"Dr. Heather," said Brimah, shyly. "Dr. Heather, *kushe!*"

Heather, almost six feet tall, towered over him.

"Hey, Brimah," she said gently, and bent down to be closer to his size. "It's great to see you, buddy!" Then she hugged him for a long time.

Brimah got to work helping us unload our luggage. Steven had his concerned look again.

"I will do it for you."

"No way, man!" Nathan had patted Steven on the back. "We're helping, brother."

Two smaller boys raced around the corner of the house. Two little round sunny faces.

"White Boy! City Boy!" Heather ran toward them, lifting them one after the other in her arms.

"Did she say 'White Boy'?" I asked Janet, after she'd hugged them, too.

"Yes, and City Boy. That's what they call them."

"But those aren't their names, really?"

She shrugged.

"These guys are awesome!" said Heather, holding their hands and sitting them next to her on the bench. "These guys are where it's at! You will see them everywhere! You guys are awesome!" They swung their legs and smiled, as though they knew she was right.

Then two girls walked tentatively in front of the porch. They were older than Brimah.

"Hi, Binty! Hi, Maria!"

"Hello, Nurse Janet." Their voices were soft. Then they smiled, looking down at the dirt of the yard.

"Come on for a hug, girls!" said Janet, waving them up the stairs. They walked together, as though attached. Janet whispered something to them as she hugged them, and they giggled.

Children on the porch

"Hello, girls," called Heather from the bench.

"Hello, Dr. Heather." They perched next to White Boy.

Slowly, as we unpacked, more children started to arrive. They seemed content to stand and watch us. Some climbed onto the bench to peek through the plastic slats that blocked the windows of our kitchen and common room. From inside, we could see their hands cupped around the sides of their faces as they pressed in to get a better view.

This morning, so far, it is just Pa Brimah, the goats, and me. I can see, far off in the distance, people walking along what I assume is another path. They must be going to work.

"Let's go, guys!" Heather is calling from inside. "We can't be late. This is a big deal."

We are going to be presented to the Primary Chief. We are not allowed to stay in Kamakwie without his approval.

I am curious. I hadn't imagined this.

L.A. is the nurse in charge of the Kamakwie Hospital, and he will take us. Brimah Samura has returned to Makeni, a city a few hours from here. Although he grew up in Kamakwie, he lives in Makeni with his family now. He will come back to bring us to the airport at the end of our stay. In the meantime, we still have Steven.

Nathan walks around the side of the house.

"Hey, where were you?" I ask.

"Looking around. I just saw Steven. He's staying up at the house where Brimah Samura was before. He said Brimah Samura's relatives have been there since, like, six this morning looking for him."

"Why?"

"I guess they come and see Brimah Samura when he's in Kamakwie, looking for money because they know he has this job. Anyway, Steven says they won't believe that Brimah Samura is gone. 'We know he's in there somewhere!' they said to him."

"Was he upset?"

"Steven? Nah. He says they'll probably keep coming back until Brimah Samura is in town again."

"Wow."

"Janet! Janet, we're going!" Heather is impatient as she steps out onto the porch with Jennifer.

L.A. seems nervous. He talks little as he leads us to an open hut with a thatched roof. The floor is cement, inlaid in places with large tiles.

We sit down. Chairs and benches are set closely together in a large circle inside the empty room. They begin to fill up. Each person who arrives shakes hands with everyone else in the circle. Heather, Janet, Jennifer, and I are the only women.

"What are all the people here for?" I whisper to L.A.

"Some are advisors to the Primary Chief. The others are people who have matters they would like the Primary Chief to settle."

"What does he settle? What kinds of things?"

"Anything that people have questions about. Sometimes quarrels. Sometimes other problems."

"How do you get to be the Primary Chief?"

"The Primary Chief is chosen from the chief-worthy families. He will be chief until he dies."

The Primary Chief walks in. He is a handsome, commanding presence — tall, assured. He wears a round, striped kufi cap and a long white tunic. He places a notebook, glasses case, and cell phone in a neat row in the center of the small wooden table in front of him.

We are first. L.A. stands up and speaks quickly.

"These are friends from North America who have come to help at the hospital. Dr. Heather is the leader of this group. She will introduce each person."

He sits down, and breathes out.

People look at us curiously as Heather speaks.

"Thank you to Mr. L.A. Conteh," says the Primary Chief when she is finished. L.A. nods. "And thank you, Dr. Heather. Your team is welcome in this chiefdom. The work you are proposing to do . . . " He stops mid-sentence. An older man with a white beard wanders in.

"The Secondary Chief," L.A. whispers to me before I can ask.

The Secondary Chief shakes hands with everyone around the circle. My hand is small in his. His eyes, when he looks down at me, are merry. He is also dressed in white, but the fabric is elaborately embroidered eyelet. He sits next to the Primary Chief, who continues his short welcoming speech.

Now the Secondary Chief speaks. "We need help. Yet the most important thing, the greatest benefit, is in training our people to run their own programs." He looks at each of the five of us. "We have intelligent people here who just need to be given proper skills."

I see some of the men nodding in agreement.

I notice one in particular, sitting close to the Primary Chief. He wears jeans and a dark gray T-shirt. He looks to be in his early thirties — my age. He seems so familiar — so North American. I feel like I should be running into him at the grocery store or the movies at home instead of here.

The Secondary Chief is finished. He sits down and smiles at us.

We leave so that the chiefs can begin their regular business and L.A. can get back to the hospital. As I step off the floor and onto the road, I look back at the man in the jeans.

Heather comes up beside me and we follow the others.

"It's funny how we end up in such different places," I say. "Just by chance, you know? You're just *born* somewhere."

"I know."

Kids start to swirl around us, running from their houses.

"Look at all these *pekins*," says Heather, using the Krio word for "kids." She reaches for her camera. "Hey, Jenn! Look at you with those *pekins*!"

Three kids grip Jenn's hands — two on one, one on the other — and are walking happily along.

"It's good that you're here," says Heather, turning to me. "It's going to be great."

THE MAMAS

I am supposed to meet up with L.A. in the hospital. I walk down from the bunkhouse. A little girl wearing a pink dress walks up the path toward me. She carries a large white bucket on one arm. She has tied a doll to her waist with a piece of red fabric with blue butterflies on it.

Everyone carries babies here. They are wrapped snugly against the small of their mothers' backs. I love to see them peeking out, watching the action around them.

The hospital is several small green-and-white buildings made of concrete block. They are joined together by open-air hallways that are usually teeming with people. Mostly women in long dresses, their heads wrapped in beautiful scarves. The main entrance has a door that is watched by a porter named Moli. He is an older man who wears a brown uniform. He sits on a wooden chair and opens the door as soon as he sees me approach. He smiles when I say, "*Kushe.*" His shoulders hunch up and his eyes twinkle, as though it is our private joke.

"Here," says L.A. He is wearing a purple-patterned hospital scrub shirt. He is probably in his forties. He is friendly, but busy. When he speaks, his words come out quickly. I like how he draws out certain syllables, his voice sliding slightly up at the ends. He opens the door to a narrow room with an extremely high ceiling. It is empty except for a wooden desk, two chairs, and a wooden bookshelf with nothing on it. There is a window at one end that looks out onto the front of the hospital grounds.

"I will give you the key to this room, and you can use it for your interviews. The Alpha ward is just beside you. No one will bother you here."

"Thank you, L.A."

He leaves. I don't close the door behind him. The room is hot.

I unfold a sheet of paper Heather gave me this morning. On their last trip to Kamakwie, she and Janet interviewed a group of women in a nearby village called Kakissy. Heather wanted to know what she should be raising money for back home. What did these women think Kakissy needed the most? This was the report. I sit in the chair next to the window to read it.

A small *pekin*, with her mama and sister, peeks at me in our yard.

The first thing the women said they needed was a birth house — a safe place for them to have their babies. They had to walk more than four miles to get to a hospital.

The second was help for their school. On Heather's report, it says:

School: There are holes in the roof, there are no benches; there is a dirt floor. There are no textbooks. There are no teaching manuals. There are only two teachers for 175 children.

I scan the rest of the report. At the bottom is a list of the women with whom they spoke. I breathe in sharply.

Sentho has had thirteen children, eight are alive and five are dead. The children died of dysentery, malaria, and other infectious diseases.

Adama has had seven children. Two are dead. They had problems because they were premature.

Kadiatu has had eight children. Five are alive; three are dead. One died of cholera and malnutrition, one died of measles, and one died of an unknown cause.

Yeabu has had ten children. One died of causes unknown.

Mbule has had seven children, and one died, possibly of malaria.

Yenoh has had thirteen children. Five died of malaria.

Konie has had seven children. One died of measles.

Kondey has had five children. One died — premature.

Sallay has had eight children. None of them has died.

I feel like I am reading the beginning of a very sad math problem. How many children are there altogether who are still alive? How many have died? What percent of the children who died had malaria? Which mother lost the most children?

And then the questions you can't answer using numbers. Do the children whose brothers and sisters are dead laugh as often as Sallay's children? Or do Sallay's children live in the fear that one of them will die soon? Do you cry as much when you lose the second brother? The third sister? Or does it get easier?

I can't think it does.

I put the paper down.

Malaria. I have a bed net hanging over my cot in the bunkhouse to keep mosquitoes away. I took antimalarial drugs before I left.

I am staring absent-mindedly into the hallway when I see L.A.'s purple shirt. He smiles on his way past.

"L.A.!" I call. "L.A.!" I go to the door.

"Yes?"

"L.A., do you have a minute? Can I ask you something?"

"Yes, of course."

"L.A., children are sick from malaria here. Can it not be treated?"

"Malaria? Yes."

"Aren't there bed nets?"

"Ah. Yes. The problem." He pauses. He pulls out one of the chairs and sits down. "The problem is that most time they are used by the mother and father. They are not used by the children as often if there is only one net for the family. There are not enough nets. But also, we have a problem with standing water. People have their water in buckets and tubs outside their houses. These are the breeding grounds for mosquitoes."

"Oh. Because there are no taps."

L.A. looks at me, puzzled.

"The water comes from a well. They have to collect the water."

"Yes. The well or the river."

"But when the kids get sick, why don't they just come to the hospital?"

"Here, it is difficult for parents. They have to work. Sometimes they leave the kids for days while they work. Not when they are breast-feeding. Then the baby is with them. But when the child is older, the children do a lot of their own care. They find their own food, sometimes. The parents, especially at the time when they are working on their farms, must work without a break. They can miss the signs of illness.

"Also, one of the primary signs of malaria is a fever. The drug peddlers will go to the field selling pills. But they do not know what the drugs do, or which is good for what problem. They just sell pills and say it will help the kid. Then, if something happens to the child because of an overdose or an incorrect medicine, they will attribute it to something else."

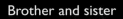
Brother and sister

L.A. in the Alpha ward

I am shocked.

"They just give them anything?"

"Yes, this is true. Drugs are not controlled in our country."

I remember reading about the drugs used by soldiers during the war.

"L.A., were you here during the war?"

The question slips out before I think.

"I escaped to Guinea when the rebels came here. I hid in the bush and then walked to Guinea to the refugee camps. I walked for about thirty days, hiding in the bush. There are some people who stayed here, though. J.B.T. is one of them. He was here. He could not leave. He was walking home when the rebels came. They forced people to stay. The rebels took over the hospital. They were here for about two years."

He pauses and looks at me. He hits the back of his chair. "When they were here, they burned the chairs like this for firewood. When the chairs were finished, they went to the beds. When the beds were finished, they went to the doors. Where you are living right now — they took off all the doors from the rooms and used them as firewood to cook. There are still the rebels here now."

"What?"

"They are here still. Everyone has gone home to their lives again."

"You are all together again?"

"Yeees. It was very difficult to believe this would one day happen. In that war, none of us could trust each other. For example, I saw you set fire to my village and you wanted to kill me, and then the war ends — and that is the only reason you didn't kill me — and now I see you today, living together with me."

"It's hard to believe, L.A., that people are living together peacefully again. I don't know if North Americans could do that."

"By God's grace."

He stands up and pushes the chair toward the desk. "I must go now." He straightens the stethoscope draped across his shoulders, smiles, and leaves.

PICTURE BOOKS

Shortly after we arrive, Janet, Heather, Nathan, and Jennifer cover one of our tables with bracelets and hair barrettes, hacky sacks and crayons, stuffed toys and puzzles, candies and gum, a soccer ball.

"Check out this anatomy puzzle," says Heather laughing. "Awesome! We're going to train some doctors here!"

I didn't bring toys. Just books. Picture books. They weighed heavy in my luggage.

I unpack them early one afternoon. There are only about ten kids on the porch. I could read to the young ones, maybe.

I walk out with a stack of books.

The kids watch me. Then they talk to each other in Krio, shaking their heads. They make room for me on the bench. One of the littlest children reaches out and touches a cover, and then pulls his finger back and laughs.

"What kind of books are these?" asks one of the older boys.

"Picture books."

"Picture books? Ahhhheee. Look at this!"

One of the books is the story of Noah's Ark. I open it.

The children stare. They are confused.

"Look at this dog! This is a dog!" one cries out.

"Where?"

The child points to the dog.

"It is the sun, there. That is what this ball is, isn't it?"

"Yes, that is the sun."

The kids begin laughing and pointing, calling out the names of things as they learn to decipher the pictures.

"Have you not seen books like this before? Is there no library at your school?"

"What is that?"

"A place full of books."

A little girl with a gift from Heather

Abu reads to us on the porch

"No! Who has such a place?"

"We have them in North America. Everywhere."

"Ahhh."

The kids are watching me.

"Would you like to hear the story? Would you like me to read the book?"

"Ah! Yes! Yes!"

I read them the Noah's Ark story, and a book with pictures of Canada, and a book about a girl whose grandfather carves her a flute.

By the time I finish, other kids have rounded the corner to our porch, and run to see what we are doing. Brimah is here. So are Binty and Maria.

When I finish, one of the oldest boys, who is crouching next to me, stands up.

"I can read this book."

He is about fifteen and wears a red shirt. He is lanky and moves easily. He reaches for it.

"Please, I would like to try to read it. I can read in English."

His smile is wide and confident.

"I would love that. Here." I hand him the book. Jenn is near and goes to find him a chair. He sits, spreading the book on his lap. And, bending low over it, he reads. The kids are delighted. He rarely stumbles, and when he does he laughs and says, "Please help me with this word. I do not know this mysterious word!" He is not frustrated or embarrassed. He wants to learn.

When he finishes, he closes the book. The children begin to drift down to the yard.

"What is your name?" I ask.

"I am Abu."

"Abu, I am Kathleen. I am happy to meet you."

We shake hands.

"Come back again."

"I will."

He hops off the porch, not bothering with the stairs.

JENN'S TALK

"We've got to keep people from getting sick in the first place," says Heather when I ask her to tell me what is causing so many people to die so young in Kamakwie.

"First, there isn't much food. There are no grocery stores, obviously. And no power, as you know — so no refrigeration. Most people get one meal a day if they are lucky, and that can depend on the time of year. They try to have rice every day.

"And then there are simple things that they don't know about that we can teach them — like how to balance their meals with foods from each of the food groups. That would cut back on malnourishment and help them fight diseases. It's not just that they don't have enough to eat, but that they aren't eating a variety of foods. The importance of washing your hands with soap. That's another one. Even just drinking clean water — a lot of people get their water from the rivers where they also wash themselves. Or if they get good water from the well, they leave it in open containers on the ground where it gets contaminated. They need to boil the water. Easier said, though, because they have to collect the wood to start a fire to do it."

Heather rarely speaks seriously for a long time. She is too impatient. She doesn't want to talk about the problems. Once she understands them, she wants to get busy fixing them. This morning is no different.

"Just come with us to the village and see Jenn's talk," she says to me. "Nath! Jenn! Janet! Ready? Let's go! Hey!" She turns back and looks at me. "How much water have you had today? I'm not treating anyone for dehydration. That's something you can prevent. Bring more water with you. Does everyone have their water?" she yells. "I'm not treating you all for dehydration!" Then she heads out the front door.

I hear her a split second later calling out happily, "Steven! Brother! *Kushe!* Ready? We have to pick up nurse Adama on the way. She's going to translate for us."

The beginning of Jenn's talk

Outside of Kamakwie there are many villages — collections of houses swirling off the dirt road. This one has a mosque and a church. The houses are close together, long grass roofs sweeping low to the ground on some, rusting corrugated metal roofs on others. Steven pulls up to a group of benches that form a semicircle in the shade of leafy trees. I stand behind the benches with Janet. Heather sets up the video camera she has with her on a tripod. Jenn and Nathan begin to unroll the laminated posters Jenn made showing pictures of how to keep kids healthy.

Adama is dressed in bright pink hospital scrubs. She is the midwife at the hospital. She stands near the truck, talking to someone from the village. The benches begin to fill with women holding babies. I watch Jenn. I like her a lot. She is quiet but funny. She has been to Africa before, although this is her first trip to Sierra Leone. She cares a lot about medicine. She brightens up when she talks about it, and I know she has worked really hard to make the presentation good. I wonder if she is nervous. Nathan stands beside her, smiling at everyone. He is going to hold the posters.

Jenn starts to speak. Adama translates. More people crowd around. Not just women now, but men, too, lifting children off the ground high in their arms. Toddlers crawl around adults' legs. One little girl wanders through the center of the circle. Some older kids run around us, playing. Others stand, tired, behind their mothers. When they have no shirts, I can see their ribs.

"Do you see the light-colored hair? It looks blonde or orange in spots?" Janet whispers to me. "That's a sign of malnourishment. So is the skin flaking from their cheeks."

"If you have meat, feed your baby before you feed yourself. The children need the protein in the meat more than you do," Jenn says.

"Before their fathers?" a man calls out.

"Yes! Kids first."

A dad keeps his baby close as he listens to Jenn

Everyone in the circle starts to laugh. I see some of the younger mothers leaning over to one another and whispering. "It is safe to feed the children bananas. Bananas will not hurt your children. They are healthy, healthy food. They can eat eggs, too. Eggs are very good for children."

Jenn had told me earlier that bananas and eggs were considered taboo for children.

People ask questions. Tentatively at first, but then as though they are hungry for the information.

"We have been having a debate here," says one man, standing up. "Should we have our latrine near the well or far from the well? What is your best advice?"

I am struck by how earnest he is.

Janet stands next to me. She pulls a long blue-and-red measuring tape from her bag and flips it expertly over her shoulders. "Now it's my turn," she tells me. "This is my part. Let's see if these kids are malnourished."

Jenn finishes, and Nathan and Janet pull the heavy white infant scale off the truck and onto the ground. Babies are shuttled to the front. Janet measures the top of their arms. Nathan and Adama weigh them. The babies seem to hate the scale and scream when Nathan tries to balance them on it. Sometimes it is hard to tell who the parents are. When a baby cries, the three or four people nearest try to calm him. Everyone crowds around to see what the child's weight is.

Weighing babies

There are two young girls standing off a little from the crowd, balancing babies on their hips. They can't be more than sixteen years old. They have booklets in their hands. Heather wanders over.

"What do you have, girls?"

Immunization records. They have them neatly filled in. They show them proudly, as though they are homework assignments.

"Great job, girls," says Heather, stroking the head of one of the babies. "Great job."

I stand back, out of the way. The sun is getting low as the afternoon melts away. There is a line of people coming down the main road with what look like hoes in their hands. I think of L.A. Back from the farm.

Eventually, the scale is loaded on the truck again, and people begin to wander home. Janet comes over to me.

"Hey there, Mama J." I smile at her. She is clearly excited. Happy to have been here. "How's it look?"

"Well, there are kids we need to see for sure," she says. She wipes her hand against her forehead and then runs it through her short, curly hair. "But it could have been worse."

"Did you tell them to come to the hospital?"

"Yes."

"Will they, do you think?"

"Don't know. We'll see."

One of the girls who showed Heather her baby's immunization record

ABU KAMARA

It is nighttime. Mama J and I are in our room. There is no power tonight. The hospital generator is off, as it usually is. We use our headlamps to see. I am writing. She is reading.

There is a knock at our door. I look up.

"Who is it?" Mama J calls.

"I am looking for Kathleen," says a boy's voice.

"Who is it?" she repeats.

"I am Abu Kamara."

"Abu?"

The voice is not Abu's. I take off my headlamp and go to the door.

I step out onto the porch. I can see the white of Pa Brimah's T-shirt beyond the edge of the porch. He is watching. The boy, dressed in a navy blue sweatshirt, stands in front of me. It is a different Abu, older by a few years than the one from our porch. He is holding an exercise book in one hand. I cannot tell what is in the other.

Abu Kamara

"Kathleen?" he says.

"Yes." I begin to feel uneasy. How does he know my name? I'm sure I haven't seen him before.

"For you."

He hands me a small, folded-up piece of paper.

"Thank you," I say.

He nods, and then he leaves.

I take it inside and put my headlamp back on.

On the front of the paper are his initials, *A.K.*

I unfold it. It is torn from a small notebook. He has written a letter neatly in blue ballpoint pen.

> *Dear my friends, I say hello to you.*
> *Please help me for my December school fees. I have not had anything for this happy day I was attending WCSL Primary School in Kamakwie. But I do not have a mother. So please help me. If you help me God will bless you from this world to the next world. So my name is Abu Kamara. I was in Class Four. This is just a small letter for you to read. So this is the end of the letter. Goodbye. Tomorrow, please don't forget. Please, please. I need money like you people.*

Nothing is scratched out. I wonder how many drafts he had to write to get it perfect. How many pieces of paper he used.

"That's a bit weird, isn't it, Janet? How did he find me?"

"Everyone knows we're here."

"I wish he hadn't asked me. It's kind of rude. It kind of puts me on the spot, doesn't it? I don't even know him."

Janet puts down her book.

"He's not trying to do that. Don't worry. We'll be meeting with Mr. Bangura, the headmaster at the school, this week. We'll sort out paying for the kids' school fees then."

I fold up the note. I can see how evenly Abu Kamara had creased it, making sixteen identical squares. The front is brown with dust where he had held it in his hand. I tuck it into my backpack.

THE ALPHA CLINIC

Marie reminds me of an old doll — the kind whose hair sticks straight up and can no longer be brushed flat. The kind that has just the underwear left on because you've given all of its nice clothes to the dolls with better hair. The kind that is grubby from being forgotten on the ground, against the wall, under the bed.

I'm not sure how old she is. Most people I meet in Kamakwie don't know their birthdays. She looks about six. Her arms are impossibly thin near her shoulders; her legs are swollen and covered in dying skin. The sides of her mouth are scarred with sores and the remains of sores.

She lies in the Alpha ward of the hospital, next to my interview room. An extraordinarily cute baby named Mohammed is in the bed next to her. When I picked Mohammed up the first time, he pooped on me. Then he grinned, and I fell in love.

"You can poop on me any day, Mohammed," I said as his mortified mother desperately tried to help me clean off my skirt. He just sat on his bed in his little red shirt and watched, smiling away at us both.

Mohammed is too young to talk, but it feels like he could. His big, round brown eyes tell stories when you hold him. But picking him up is like lifting a little bird. He is delicate. Below his large belly, his legs are like pipe cleaners.

Mohammed and Marie and the other children in the Alpha ward are there because they are malnourished. They are not getting enough nutrients from their food; they are not getting enough food. They are not growing properly. They cannot fight diseases.

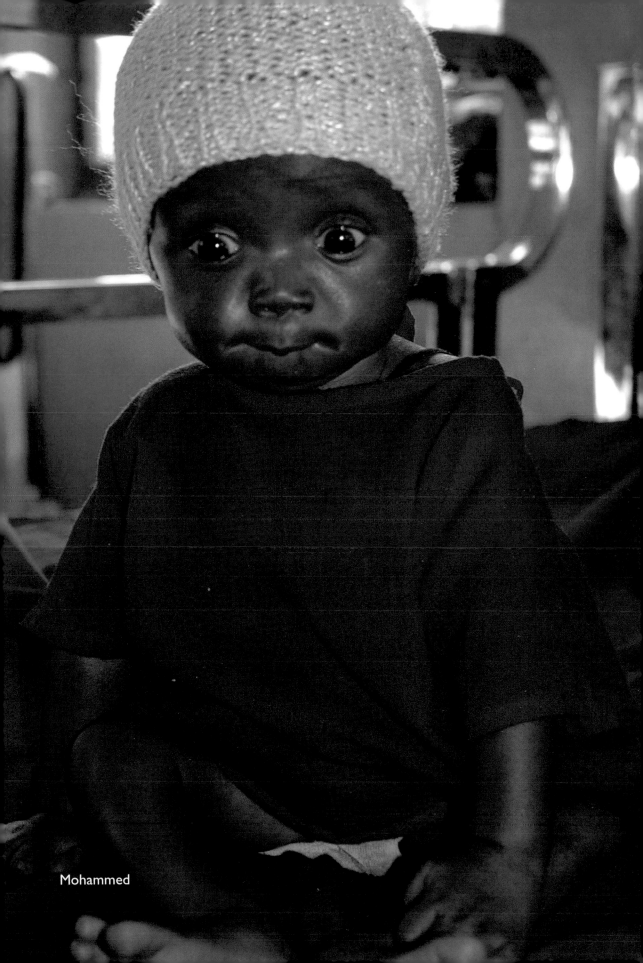

Mohammed

The first time Heather and Janet visited the hospital in Kamakwie, they met a little boy named Alpha. He died because he was malnourished. So Heather and Janet raised money to start the Alpha Clinic here. At the Alpha Clinic, parents get free medical care for malnourished children. They hoped that would encourage people to bring their children to the hospital, people who otherwise would not have the money to pay for the weeks it takes to make their children healthy again.

"It's usually the mother who comes in with the child," says Adama, mixing up food for the children in the ward that day. Adama, I learn, is not just a nurse and the hospital midwife. She is also in charge of the Alpha Clinic. Today, she is not in pink scrubs. Today, she wears an elegant gown — navy blue with large gold, green, and white flowers embroidered all over it. She has a wide headband made from the same material tied around her forehead.

"Sometimes it is a grandmother who comes. Sometimes fathers. One time a woman walked thirty-eight miles to bring her child to the hospital when she heard about the Alpha program. Thirty-eight miles she walked with the child on her back!"

Mohammed is sitting on his mother's lap. She takes a bowl from Adama and begins to feed him. Adama hands another bowl to the mother of Foday, a little boy who looks about two years old.

"The children are usually fine while they are breast-fed," Adama continues. "It is after that there is high risk for malnutrition. The children are then running off on their own, and it is harder for the mother to see what they eat. The mother is sometimes pregnant again. Sometimes," she says as she puts a green cup of food next to Marie, "it will take two weeks for the child, once they become really sick, to get better here. Sometimes more. Sometimes less. But the parents often want to go home early. They cannot stay here with the child. They have more children to feed. They must work on their farms. So then the children leave before they are better."

I look at Marie. She lies motionless, naked except for a blue cloth tied around her waist.

"How old is she?"

"She is eight, I think."

Janet comes in.

"She has kwash," she tells me.

"Kwash?"

"Kwashiorkor. It's a kind of malnutrition. You can tell because her legs and face are so swollen." She nods toward Mohammed. "He has marasmus — the big belly and wasted arms and legs. Younger kids usually have marasmus, the older ones are kwash kids."

Adama leans over Marie and shakes her.

"Marie! Marie!"

Adama says something in Krio to Marie and then leaves the room, returning with a raspberry-colored hospital smock — a bigger version of the red one Mohammed wears.

"We had them made for the Alpha kids with some of the money," Adama says to Janet. Janet smiles. Adama shakes Marie again, and then, when Marie mumbles something in response, begins to dress her. She slips one arm in, then the other, gently, as if Marie is an infant. Marie is too tired to help her. Too tired to sit up.

"She needs to eat. She is not eating the food," says Adama.

"She has to eat," I say. "Marie, you have to eat."

"You hold her. That will help," says Adama.

I slip awkwardly behind Marie on the bed, pulling her almost lifeless body onto my lap. Her head flops forward. I hug her close to me, holding her head up against my shoulder with my hand. Adama scoops a kind of soup into her mouth with a spoon. It dribbles down her chin, leaving white wet tracks on her shirt.

I stroke her cheek.

She falls asleep again shortly. I'm not sure how much food she has eaten.

"Kathleen," says Janet, pulling me to one corner of the room after Marie lies down, "Marie is not going to live."

"Why not?"

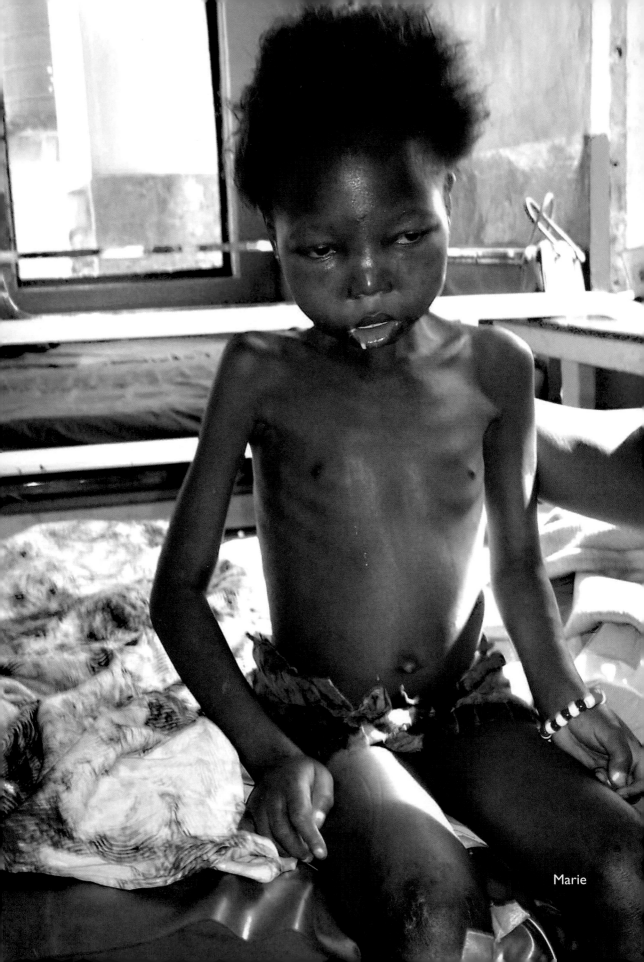

Marie

"Marie is very sick. She is going to die."

"No, she isn't."

We aren't in some movie, Mama J. Not everything here has to be depressing.

"No, she isn't," I repeat, louder.

"Kathleen, I've seen lots and lots of these kids. She is extremely sick."

"She is in the hospital. She is just hungry."

"It's more complicated than that. All of her organs are affected. Everything is affected when you don't have the proper nourishment."

She just needs help from us. I am beginning to get upset.

"I'm getting Heather," I say. "Where is Dr. Heather?"

I rush out of the room, out of the hospital. I walk back to the bunkhouse as fast as I can without running.

"Heather! Heather!" I yell. "Heather!"

She comes out of her room.

"Heather, you have to come and see this little girl. You have to help her. Janet says she is going to die. I think you just need to see her."

Heather looks at me. Jenn and Nathan have come into the common room. They look at Heather. They are worried — I assume about Marie.

Good. Maybe they will help her, then.

"Okay."

Heather walks down to the hospital. Strong, tall Heather. I know she is the answer. I can feel it.

She talks to Adama. There is only one doctor at the hospital. Dr. Emmett is a North American, too, visiting for a few months. Heather asks for his permission to examine Marie. Every patient in the hospital is his responsibility. He is glad to have Heather's help.

Heather sits next to Marie on the bed. She carefully feels her belly and looks at her arms and speaks softly to her.

Then she changes her medicine.

I knew there was something wrong that someone had just missed. I knew it.

"We'll try it," she says to me.

That night after supper, Heather, Nathan, Jenn, and Mama J sit me down on the couch.

"Kathleen," says Heather. Her usually cheery voice is serious. "Kathleen, Marie may be dead in the morning."

Not again. What is with these people? Aren't they doctors?

"I know," I say.

"Really. She might be dead. The medicine may not work. Sometimes you cannot save kids who are that sick, even if you want to."

"I know," I say.

"Even if you want to."

"Okay."

I can feel the four of them staring at me. Mama J and Nathan and Jenn start talking about what happens to your body when you don't eat properly. They give statistics about how often kids die of malnutrition around the world. They talk about other patients they have lost.

They try so hard to be kind to me, to prepare me, to help guard against my heart breaking.

I leave and go into my room. I crawl underneath the mosquito net, tucking it tightly around my mattress. I pretend to be asleep when Mama J comes in.

MARIE

The hospital staff meets early in the mornings in the long bright chapel just across from the main ward. The room is an open space, only its edges rimmed with benches. One wall is papered with pictures from the Bible. The others are windows. There is a blackboard and a podium.

Sister Ya, the hospital chaplain, moves like a lightning bolt around the room, part preacher, part pep-squad leader. I usually get such a kick out of her. I usually love watching the faces of the staff as they pray or sit in the stillness. I can feel how it helps them to be there in the morning for a few minutes together.

But I hardly notice them this morning.

Marie, Marie. I say her name over and over in my head.

When the short service is over, J.B.T. stands up. J.B.T. is a nurse and the hospital's lab technician — the one L.A. talked about, who stayed at the hospital when the rebels were here. He walks to the podium and holds up his hand, his expressive eyebrows raised high.

"We have decided to hold a Singspiration for our guests," he says. He looks pleased and turns to the blackboard, where he writes "Singspiration" in large letters.

Marie, Marie.

"It will be a contest in honor of the Christmas season. We will divide into two teams: Dr. Heather and Dr. Emmett will lead them. We will practice singing carols and then, at the end of the week, we will see which team sings them the best! I will be the judge."

Hurry up, please. Hurry up, please. It's time. It's time. Marie, Marie.

J.B.T. divides us into two groups, and people good-naturedly cross the room to sit with their teammates. I am on Dr. Emmett's team. We are to practice right then.

The first Noël the angels did say,
Was to certain poor shepherds in fields as they lay.

And then,

Hail the heaven-born Prince of Peace!
Hail the Son of Righteousness!
Light and life to all he brings,
Risen with healing in his wings.

Good God, I think. *We're singing all the verses. When will this end?*

Mild he lays his glory by,
Born that man no more may die,
Born to raise the sons of earth,
Born to give them second birth.
Hark! The herald angels sing,
"Glory to the newborn king!"

I sing, but I can't hear the words. *Hurry up!*

Finally finished. Everyone leaving through the door at once. Me, stuck toward the end, trying to let the staff out first so they can begin work. Heather and Janet beside me. Then, Heather striding out, keeping a step ahead of me, around the corner, past Moli the porter. Then, people greeting us, "*Kushe, kushe!*" Stopping to talk for a moment, trying not to seem hurried. Then down the hall, to the right, and through the doors to Alpha, Heather first, blocking my view.

Marie, Marie.

Alive!

SAINY'S FAMILY

Binty and Maria visit our porch every afternoon, smiling shyly. I rarely see them apart. They move almost as though they are attached. They are best friends and, I learn, cousins. It is hard to know much about them, though, as they don't talk a lot. I find that with most of the girls. The boys talk and tease with us. Abu is always making jokes and telling me stories, smiling his wide, catchy grin.

But the girls are usually quiet, saying only a few words at most.

I try to interview Binty and Maria one day. Maybe if I sit down with them and ask questions, they will talk more.

"What is your favorite class in school, Binty?"

"I like maths. Language arts," she says — quietly.

"Maria, what do you like to do in school?"

"I like religious moral education."

They sit still, looking at me expectantly.

"Religious education? What is your favorite story from the Bible?"

"I like Goliath and David," says Maria.

"And what about you, Binty?"

"I like Joseph."

"And what kinds of things do you like to do outside of school?"

"Long jump," says Binty.

"Balance ball," says Maria.

"What would you like to do when you grow up, Maria?"

"Nurse."

"What about you, Binty?"

"Nurse."

"Is there anything you wonder about me?" I ask.

"Where is your mother?" asks Binty right away.

"Does she live with you?" asks Maria.

"My mother does not live with me," I say. "She lives far away from me. I don't get to see her very often. I miss her a lot, and I wish she were closer."

They smile at each other. They nod their heads. Then they get up to go.

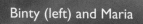
Binty (left) and Maria

Heather pokes her head in the door.

"How'd it go?"

"They're just not chatty," I say.

"You need to talk to Sainy. He's Binty's grandfather. Let's send word for him!"

Heather loves sending word for people. Some people have cell phones, but most do not. There are no land lines at all. So people send word. When we do it, one of the kids from the porch runs to find the person we want to talk to, and gives them our message.

Sainy arrives later that evening. He is seventy years old and the kindergarten teacher at the Wesleyan Church of Sierra Leone School. He is slight in his oversized button-down shirt, but his arms are lined with muscles. He has intelligent eyes, and he smiles while he speaks.

"You met with Binty today," he begins.

"Yes, I did. She is your granddaughter?"

"Yes. She lives in my home. Binty's mother was given children, but they all died at birth. She would deliver them, and they would not live long. This happened six times."

"Oh, Sainy. I'm so sorry to hear that. How awful for your daughter."

"She is my sister."

"Isn't Binty your granddaughter?"

"Yes. The daughter of my sister."

I remembered then that Mama J had told me that families in Sierra Leone do not separate nieces and nephews, daughters and sons, uncles and aunts, the way we usually do in North America.

"I'm so sorry for your sister."

"When Binty was born, I went to my sister in the village where she lives. Twenty miles I went on foot to collect Binty from her."

"You took Binty away?"

"Yes, I had a dream and the Lord spoke to me and said I should help my sister. But my sister did not want me to take Binty. Binty was her only daughter. She had only one other child, a son.

"'Do not take my daughter from me,' my sister said.

Sainy

"'Sister,' I said, 'I want to do something fine for your daughter.'

"My sister had big love for me, so she did it. And she still has big love for me! When my sister comes here, she takes Binty on her lap and loves her. She is so proud of Binty! She says for me to continue with Binty because Binty is in school. Most girls don't go to school because of poverty. You need to educate the girls! You must educate girls for the strength of Sierra Leone!" Sainy's voice gets louder. He pauses for a moment. He is still smiling.

"Fortunately for me, Binty is doing well in school. The only problem with Binty is that she was bitten by a snake when she went to the farm. She stepped on a snake. A cobra."

"What happened?"

"They couldn't bring her to the hospital, so they used traditional healing. It means she is now slow at walking. But she is a smart girl. So is Mariama."

"Is that Maria?"

"Yes. She is also my granddaughter. Her grandmother is my sister as well. Maria's mother left her baby, so the grandmother, my sister, went and collected her. All the work is being done by the grandmother. She has to work hard. I used to help her, but I am not able to carry the two loads on a teacher's salary. But Mariama, too, is in school. Both girls are in school.

"Now may I tell you how we get our food?"

Sainy continues to talk into the night, explaining to me how people survive in Kamakwie and its villages by farming. They grow peanuts and cassava — which is like a sweet potato — rice and green-green, which is a kind of cabbage. A few days later, he arrives with farm tools, and has the boys from the porch show me how they are used, the cutlass, the big hoe. Everything done by hand.

Sainy is a wise man. I spend a lot of time with him while we are in Kamakwie. He is an excellent teacher, explaining things over and over to be sure I understand. His eyes twinkle when I show any interest. He teaches me how the grass roofs on the houses are made, and he organizes the kids at the school to demonstrate traditional games for me.

I love that he is proud of where he is from. I love that he walked twenty miles to give Binty a future. I have big love for Sainy.

DELIVERY

Mama J can't stay away from the hospital. The beds in the big main room are crowded with patients and their families: mothers, fathers, grandmothers, children, tiny new babies. People bring rice and plastic basins and what look like bundles of fabric, and pile them neatly next to the beds. They wait under tall windows without screens — bright rectangles of light and flies and flowers.

Mama J knows about making people feel better just by sitting with them. She perches on the ends of those beds every chance she gets. Patients speak earnestly to her in Krio and Limba and she listens hard, even when there is no translator.

She disappears down the path to the hospital in the night when the generator flicks on, sending wavery light into our bedroom. L.A. turns on the precious power for emergency operations and, sometimes, when someone is having a baby.

I think I would like to see a baby being born. Mama J says she'll check with Adama.

"Do anything they ask you right away," says Mama J, as we walk quickly to the hospital one night. She stops to catch her breath and to look directly up at me. "Don't ask why. Just do it." We pass through a door into a small room cramped with equipment and a cot. L.A. and Adama stand at the mother's bent legs. The generator hums like an insect.

"*Kushe!*" Adama waves us in. Her full-length dress is peach and flares at her ankles. It is embroidered with pink and yellow thread, the edges scalloped lace. Her head is wrapped in a matching scarf. She looks like she is ready for church.

She says something to L.A. in Krio, and then pulls her hands into pale yellow latex surgical gloves that are too big for her. She keeps changing those gloves as she helps that mother. One new, clean, too-big pair after another.

One of the large hospital wards

For a long time, I hold the mother's hand as she moans low and tired, rocking back and forth. She has been trying to have that baby for two days. Finally, her family brought her the long way into the hospital. I wonder how they got her here. Did someone have a motorbike? Did she have to walk? I rub her shoulders.

Then Adama, L.A., and Mama J begin to talk quietly to each other. I catch a few phrases about cords.

After a minute or two, Mama J comes over. "You have to go," she says.

L.A. glances at me, and then begins sorting through the equipment stacked along the wall. Adama holds her gloved hands in the air, waiting, watching me.

I kiss the woman's cheek. "I'll come see you and your baby tomorrow," I whisper. I don't know if she speaks English, but she tries to smile anyway.

Mama J hurries me out of the room. "I'll be home soon," she says, and turns back toward the delivery room. She closes the door behind her.

I wait in our bedroom. The lights click off after a while. Janet comes in a few minutes later.

"How is she? How is the baby?"

"The baby died, Kathleen."

She comes toward me. I do not want to be touched.

I walk away. I go outside. Pa Brimah waves.

I sit on the blue bench.

I think of my own babies. Of what it feels like when they are laid on your belly, newborn. Heavy and sticky. Moving.

I look up at the stars. Where is the moon? Over some other part of the sky.

I know that a lot of babies die in Sierra Leone.

I cannot help but think of the little screaming girl from our drive up. *Was I bad luck for this baby, too?*

KAKISSY SCHOOL

Kakissy village school is not like any school I've seen before. The long, rectangular building is more the idea of a school. It has mud brick walls enough to hold up the corrugated roof, but only

A Kakissy classroom

Just as the kids are settled, I see Heather running across the field toward me.

"Kathleen, there are no pens!" she yells.

"What?" She is closer now.

"No pens! There are no pens!"

"Well, pencil is fine, then."

Heather laughs nervously.

"No pencils. Nothing to write with."

Saidu comes over to us.

"Saidu, don't these children have things to write with?"

A pained expression flits across his face. I can see how much he wants this to work. "No," he says slowly. "No, not at this school."

I look at the Storytelling kids. They hold their pieces of paper, watching them rustle in the breeze. I look at the school building. I can see Jenn looking at me from the half-window. Nathan stands next to her. I look over at Janet's group, off by the trees, expecting to see her wandering toward me, too.

"I just assumed they'd have something to write with. I thought maybe they might need extra paper, but how on earth do they go to school with no pens?"

I try to think. I can see the Chief of Kakissy sitting by the chickens. I can see the groups of parents milling around. And then oddly, I see the kids in Janet's group bending over their papers.

Mama J looks up at us, and smiles. She pats her giant brown bag.

"Excuse me, Saidu."

Heather and I run across the grass. Reverend Alusine is helping Janet. He is tall and wears an elaborate golden shirt. He looks at me and laughs. "Com-mu-ni-ty!" he begins to chant, playfully. "Com-mu-ni-ty! Look at our group working here! Look at this fine group of kids!"

Mama J reaches into her bag and produces from its depths a big box of crayons.

We break the crayons in half and divide them up between the groups. Mama J finds a few pens in her bag, and we collect others from Reverend Alusine, Reverend Morris, and Saidu.

One of the boys in my Storytelling group

The kids, thankfully, seem happy with what we have.

They work hard at their papers, big kids helping the smaller ones. The teachers take the papers at the end of the afternoon to keep them safe until our next visit later in the week. The kids swarm around the yard, many clutching their bits of crayon.

As we walk through the crowd of them to the truck, I notice a little girl holding her mother's hand, sobbing.

"Oh, what's wrong?" I bend down low to see her.

"She has lost her crayon," says her mother. "She has dropped it in the grass and it is gone."

I have only a white crayon left in my bag. I hadn't given it out. White crayons never seem to me to be of much use.

I give it to the little girl. She holds it tightly in her hand. She smiles. She jumps on the spot.

"*Thankee! Thankee!*"

Sometimes the white crayon is the best one in the box.

BANANA TREE

"Okay, so the group we really want to beat is over there." I point to where I can see Mama J's back in the distance. Reverend Alusine is beside her. Today he is meticulously dressed in a tie and a tan trench coat. "There by that banana tree."

I stand where the low green plants that cover the ground near Kakissy school break into the dirt soccer field. We are finishing our second visit to the school, and plan to end with a cheering contest between the groups.

Abu Sesay is one of the older boys in my Storytelling crew. His story, "Cat and Rat," is in his hand. Now he is perplexed.

"The banana tree?"

"Yes, the banana tree. Right there."

"That is not a banana tree."

I hold onto one of the goalposts — made from a slender tree trunk — and shield my eyes from the sun.

"Well, then, the tree that looks like a banana tree."

Abu Sesay starts to giggle.

"That tree does not look like a banana tree."

One of his friends wanders over to catch the joke. A girl, not much older than they are — maybe fourteen — comes, too. She stops a few feet away. She has an infant in her arms.

"I thought banana trees were short and kind of stocky, with palm leaves on them," I say.

"Banana trees don't have palm leaves! They have banana leaves!" Both boys are laughing now.

"Well, they look like palm leaves, don't they?"

"No."

The field at Kakissy school. The Storytelling kids are on the left. Reverend Alusine's Community group is in the distance under the trees.

"Okay. Isn't that a palm tree?" I point to a tall tree with a light trunk. Now there is a group of kids standing near me.

"Coconut!" they yell.

"But it looks like a palm tree."

"No, it doesn't!"

"That," says Abu Sesay, grinning, "is a palm tree."

And he points to a tree that looks, I swear, exactly like the coconut tree. Unless you are used to finding your food in the trees. Then, I suppose, it looks exactly like a palm tree.

I am laughing now, too. "I just want to be louder than Reverend Alusine's group. He thinks he can win."

Abu Sesay runs back over to where Saidu has gathered the rest of our group for a practice.

"Storytelling!" they call out. "Story-telling!"

A little boy dressed in orange jumps and claps his hands, beaming.

"Louder! Louder!" says Saidu.

Then all five groups gather in front of the Kakissy chief.

"Health-y foods! Hygiene!" they chant. "Story-telling!"

Heather jumps up and down in front of her group, clapping her hands and leading them with her booming voice. "Things we do! Things we do!"

Reverend Alusine runs in front of his kids, waving his hands. "We will be the loudest! Com-mu-ni-ty! Com-mu-ni-ty!"

"Story-telling!" our *pekins* shout back at him. "Story-TELLING!"

Sometimes the kids laugh so hard that they can hardly speak. But then they yell again, their happy voices soaring up into the bright sky.

AGAIN

I stand on the edge of the porch looking up at the moon in the quiet. I have just finished a phone call home.

"Kathleen!"

I jump.

Abu Kamara appears out of the darkness.

"Kathleen!"

"Yes, Abu."

"Did you read my letter?"

"Yes."

He stands, waiting.

I don't know what to say.

"I read it, Abu."

Why does he keep at me like this? I don't know if he is the right person to give money to. What about the other kids?

"I read it. I will answer in a few days, Abu. I'm not sure what to do."

"Okay. Okay. I will be back."

"No, no. Don't come back. You don't need to come back."

"Okay." His voice sounds tense. It is dark, so I cannot easily read his expression.

And then he is gone.

WHAT NATHAN SAW

Nathan and I walk together through the Kamakwie market. The wooden stalls are packed closely together, their awnings blocking out the light and making the narrow walkways between them feel like a maze. There are piles of shoes, bolts of fabric, baby clothes, plastic buckets. The food market is in a separate section, up a set of stairs on a wide concrete pad. It smells of fish.

"A woman brought in a dead three-year-old yesterday," Nathan tells me. Little kids duck out from underneath tables, flashing smiles at us as we walk by.

Nathan often goes on hospital rounds, visiting patients with Dr. Emmett and the other nurses.

"A little girl. The mother put her body on the bed. When we confirmed that the girl was dead, the mother just picked her back up. You know how they take the little kids by the arm to sling them over their back? That's just what she did. As though the little girl were alive. She wrapped a cloth around the child to hold her on, and just left."

How awful the hard, dead cold must have felt against her back as she walked, who knows how far, to bring her daughter home. How different from when it was a warm child snuggled next to her — a little head looking round the side of her chest.

That made four dead babies and one dead toddler in seven days. That we knew of.

Beloved child

JOY

I am surprised by the joy in Kamakwie.

In the midst of so much death, so much hunger, so much missing, people laugh and dance and smile, smile, smile.

At first, I notice the smiles because of my camera.

"Click, click! Click, click!" people call when I walk through town.

When I stop to take a photograph, someone else often pulls at my elbow.

"Click me! Click me!"

On our porch, kids jump up from the bench to try and get into the frame of my photograph, pushing each other good-naturedly out of the way.

I click and then, from all angles, people come, forming a tight circle around me, laughing and shrieking delightedly at the image on the back of my digital camera.

One afternoon, we stop in to visit Pa Sorie on our way into town for a bottle of Fanta soda. Pa Sorie is the oldest man in Kamakwie. Mama J brings a photograph of him from her last visit.

"I didn't forget," she says, waving it as he steps out of his house.

"Pa Sorie — *kushe!*" Heather gives him a bear hug.

Resplendent in an emerald green tunic and a shimmering golden kufi cap, Pa Sorie moves to a chair outside. Children circle around him as he talks, joking with us and with him. Old people are honored in Kamakwie. Living long is something to celebrate. It does not happen often enough.

After a few moments, I notice a group of teenaged girls standing shyly near the mango tree whose feathery leaves shade Pa Sorie's yard. They are looking at my camera. I take a photo of one of them. They giggle as they crowd around to see it. I watch their faces and see the girl in the photograph stop smiling. She is confused. The others lean into one another happily. She is still.

Pa Sorie

"It's you! It's you!" her friend says, pulling the camera gently upward. "It's you!"

Then the girl in the photo covers her mouth and begins to laugh. She bends close to learn what her own pretty face looks like. She nods at it, satisfied.

I learn how to look, too. I learn to see joy like a color around me.

One Sunday morning, I wander with Jenn off the main Kamakwie road, through the lanes between the houses. We come upon White Boy, bare feet, short purple pants, and eyes still sleepy in the half-light. He is in front of a long building, its blackened cement walls covered with notes people have made with chalk. It looks as if someone has been working out a series of algebra problems. *R=17*, it says on the pillar. Then, beside the closed, windowless plank door: *R=17/9*. Right behind White Boy's head, children have been drawing on the wall, leaving large blue scribbles.

White Boy isn't interested in the wall, though. He is watching two of the older boys play tetherball. They whack the ball with all their might, their legs spinning up on the follow-through, calling out as the rope wraps around the pole. White Boy jumps with each hit as if he imagines himself playing, too. The pole is a tall stick planted securely in the ground. The ball, tied to a yellow rope, is a bag full of dirt. But in full flight, it is a blur of strength.

On another day, we take the main road out of Kamakwie. Every now and again we see people walking along the sides, usually in single file, two or three together. They step out of the bush onto the road, or turn off the road into the bush along a path I cannot see.

After a little while, a boy wearing only dark blue cut-off sweatpants and yellow plastic shoes appears. He carries a long, thin piece of wood over his shoulder. He is probably twelve and he walks by himself in the quiet. We drive slowly, and I watch him. He is gloriously alone. What a gift in the sunshine, clouds sweeping the sky. When we pass him, he looks up, shaken from his thoughts. His fingers rest lightly on his stick as though playing an instrument. He smiles.

White Boy watches the tetherball game

The dancers at the party

And then there is Dr. Heather's drumming party. She is determined to have one. People play hand drums all over Sierra Leone. Dr. Heather bought one in the Freetown market for herself so she could learn.

"I might get Brimah to teach me," she says. Brimah loves to play. He looks longingly at the drum when he visits us, his eyes fixed on it in the corner of our common room. He never asks to use it. But when Heather brings it to him, he shines.

"I talked to some of the *pekins*," says Heather enthusiastically as she scoops potato leaf soup onto rice at lunch. "They're going to hook us up with some drummers and some dancers. This is going to be awesome!"

I come up from the hospital one afternoon to find dozens of people spilling over our porch and onto the grounds around it. There are five official dancers, their faces outlined in thick strokes of white paint. Two wear shoes, two are in bare feet, and the youngest dances in blue knee socks. They move in time with the drums, concentrating on the rhythms, stirring the dust and stones as they step.

Mothers from the Alpha Clinic heard the sound of the drums from inside their hospital room and followed it up the hill. They watch at the edges of the audience, babies peeking round them. Every once in a while, one of them enters the dance. Sometimes she rests her hand on the shoulder of one of the boys, directing him, helping him interpret the beat with his body.

I stand next to one of the mothers.

"We dance," she tells me, "because there is peace in our land. We cannot stop ourselves."

I count four drums. The paint is almost worn off the sides of the biggest. It was once light blue. Two boys have smaller green drums dotted with black. The bottom of one is cracked off. The goatskin stretched tightly across the top of the other is torn, a large piece of it missing where fingers have slapped for so long. The boy drums anyway, one-handed, on the part that remains. Another boy, his shirt open, plays using pieces of metal on a bucket with no bottom. Its sides are pockmarked and rusting in the places where it has been hit the most.

Brimah with Heather's drum

The boys drum for more than an hour without stopping. When their friends call out, they lift their arms high in the air, thumbs up.

I love to dance. I cannot resist the music. The woman next to me takes my hands and we dance together. Then the young dancers make room for Heather and Mama J, Nathan, Jenn, and me to join them. The kids on the porch laugh and point, clap and cheer.

The drummers stop to rest for a bit. And then there is Brimah on the porch with Heather's drum. He stands, balancing it between his legs, beating out intricate patterns, his face bright like the sun. People, milling around, stop to watch him. He doesn't seem to notice. Instead, he starts to sing in Krio:

> *Tell him thankee,*
> *tell him,*
> *tell Papa God thankee.*

And the *pekins* join in, their voices loud and carefree:

> *O let we give him glory,*
> *give him glory,*
> *give him,*
> *give Papa God glory.*
> *For what he do,*
> *for what he do*
> *for we,*
> *I'll go tell him thankee.*
> *What he do,*
> *for we,*
> *I'll go tell him thankee.*
> *Tell him thankee,*
> *tell him,*
> *tell Papa God thankee.*

I learn in Kamakwie that joy has nothing to do with things. Joy is a gift all of its own.

MARIE'S FAMILY

Marie is bewitched.

That's what her grandmother tells me.

At first she lost weight. They did not know why. She became very thin. Then her belly began to swell up, and her hair started to fall out.

"They do not realize that it was because of malnutrition," says Adama.

We are in my interview room. The door is closed, and Marie's grandmother looks at me from the chair beside Adama, her eyes tired underneath graceful eyebrows. Pretty lilac earrings hang near her cheeks. She does not speak English. She speaks Limba, one of the tribal languages.

"First," translates Adama, "they went to a traditional healer for herbs. They picked some leaves from the woods. They boiled them for Marie to drink."

"Did they make her better?"

"No. So Marie's father took her to a sorcerer to find out the cause of the sickness. The sorcerer said that something went wrong in the womb. He said that the mother's family were witches."

"Witches?"

"Yes. So the father and his relatives accused the mother and her relatives of witchcraft."

I have seen Marie's father. He often sits with her by himself in the mornings. I have a picture of him in a red-and-green ball cap smiling at her. In it, Marie is lying on the bed wearing a beaded bracelet from the bunch on the table in our room. She is resting her head on a black plastic bag tied up like a pillow. Someone had finally fixed her hair, twisting what remained of it into four small braids that stand up straight.

"This woman here," says Adama, "is the mother of Marie's mother."

Marie's grandmother becomes increasingly upset as she speaks to Adama.

"Marie's father accused her mother's family of wanting to kill the child."

"Where is Marie's mother?" I hadn't thought until that moment that it should have been her sitting day after day in the Alpha ward. The other Alpha kids have their mothers with them.

Marie and her father

"The mother is in another country near here. She is in Guinea. She doesn't know that Marie is sick."

Marie's grandmother speaks for a long time before Adama translates again.

"Marie went with her mother to Guinea at first," says Adama. "The father was angry. He went to the chief of the village and sued this grandmother so that she would have to send for the child. The grandmother sent to Guinea, and Marie had to come back to the care of her father."

"And it was in his care that she became ill?"

"Yes. The grandmother saw the child after she had been in the care of the father's family for a few years. She wanted to know why Marie had become so thin. She was not thin before.

"Then the father wanted to make a case against the mother's side. So he said they had witchcraft. If there is witchcraft, anything he does to care for the child is useless. So he neglected her. Then he asked the village chief to take action against the grandmother because of the witchcraft."

"What kind of action?"

"They fine you or they flog you or they bind you up and put you in the sun. They punish you."

"They beat you? The chief would do that to this grandmother?"

"Well, first, her chief advised them to bring the child to the hospital to try and cure her."

"Oh, good," I say, throwing out of my mind the image I'd conjured of Marie's grandmother bound up with rope, baking in the sun, her cheek hard against the gritty earth, her tired eyes closed tightly against the dust. "That's good news. That's a relief. Now they'll know it's malnutrition and not bewitchment."

"No. That is not how they think."

"But the grandmother understands it wasn't witchcraft that made Marie sick."

Adama asks the grandmother. The grandmother shakes her head, no.

"She cannot deny that the child is bewitched because her chief has said it."

"But Marie will be healthy because of the hospital care. How can anyone possibly think it is witchcraft?"

"They will say that the people who have bewitched her have given up the witchcraft," says Adama. "They will say that the witches have healed her in their own witch way. They are traditional people. This is their belief."

"But it's not true!"

"This is their belief."

I shake my head in frustration.

"What will happen to Marie when she leaves the hospital? Does she stay with her grandmother?"

"No. She will go back to her father."

"But what if he still believes in the witchcraft? If he hates her mother's family, what if he says she is still bewitched even if she's better? What if he neglects her again?"

"It is the tradition for her to go back with her father."

"What will happen to the grandmother?"

"She will wait for her judgment."

Our interview ends. The grandmother leaves and goes back to sit with Marie.

I stay at my desk and stare out the window. I think of Binty and Maria sitting on our blue bench, their arms wrapped around one another's shoulders. I think of the girls I see getting their hair braided by aunties in front of their houses; of the girls in town peeking out of windows and standing in dark doorways, proud in fancy dresses.

I wonder what Marie looks like when she is healthy, running in and around village houses with thatched roofs. I wonder if she has a best friend or a sister or brother waiting anxiously for her to come home. I wonder whether she has ever gone to school or if she works on the farm. I wonder what she wants in her life.

I wonder how she felt when she had to leave her mama. I wonder if she misses her, lying there in the Alpha ward, too tired to sit up.

ISOTU

Isotu is the only child on our porch that I almost never see smile.

Both of her parents were killed in the war. She is an orphan. She lives with her grandmother and her aunties.

She visits, usually alone, in the evenings after dark. She sits on the blue bench and says nothing, even if you sit and talk to her. It tries my patience.

But Mama J sits next to her, holding her hand.

"What's wrong, Isotu? What's bothering you?"

Isotu will never say.

Then one evening she starts to cry.

"My grandmother says there is no more food."

Then she runs away.

The next night, she comes back to the porch, holding a black plastic grocery bag.

"These are for you." She hands the bag to Janet and then runs away again.

It is full of unripened oranges, as if to contradict what she said the night before. She must have picked them.

Half an hour later, as we sit down for dinner, she knocks frantically at our door.

"Isotu, what is it?" I go to the door. She is clearly distressed. "Sweetie, what's wrong?"

"I need to have the bag back. I forgot to keep the bag."

It is sitting next to Nathan on the table. He hands it to her.

Then she leaves.

Mama J and Isotu

THE SOCCER BALL

Nathan sits on the arm of the couch in our common room, using a small hand pump to slowly inflate the soccer ball he brought. He squeezes the ball between his hands every few minutes to test its firmness.

"There!" he says, finally, standing up. He goes out onto the porch, balancing the ball on his palm as he closes the screen door behind him.

The instant he sees it, Abu falls to his knees.

"*Thankee*, Allah!" he cries out, bending his head and arms low to the ground. "*Thankee! Thankee!*"

There are other boys there, too, jumping high in the air, high-fiving one another and shouting, "A football! A football! Praise God!" But I can't stop watching Abu. He is often smiling, but this is different. When he lifts his face to the sky, I see boundless joy.

The soccer game. Abu is in the black jeans.

Who knew a soccer ball could matter that much to anyone?

Abu leaps suddenly to his feet and joins his friends, turning the dirt by our bunkhouse into a soccer field.

I lean against one of the black metal poles that outline the edge of the porch, and watch the game.

Kids pour around the sides of the building like iron filings drawn to a magnet, word of the ball spreading somehow through the wind.

The late afternoon sunlight fingers its way through the leaves of the mango trees on the western edge of the hospital grounds. As the boys play on, I begin to look at their feet.

Most of the boys wear plastic shoes — some flip-flops, some with buckles; one boy wears only one shoe, and several have no shoes at all. They can't notice their feet or it would be impossible to run so fast, grinding their heels into the hard dirt and sharp stones as they twist to reach the ball.

The smaller kids settle in on the sidelines. White Boy and City Boy run the short length of the yard cheering. Other children sit on the porch, their legs hanging over the edge. The kids carrying little brothers and sisters on their hips stand, some resting against the wall, chattering excitedly. Still others crowd onto the bench, laughing.

It gets close to our suppertime.

"It's time to go home!" Heather yells. "We'll organize another game with the ball later! We'll have a big football game another day!"

The boys keep playing. The kids on the porch keep talking and laughing. The darkness rises slowly.

"A great big game!" she yells half-heartedly. Jenn goes inside and gets one of the bags of candy.

"*Pekins*!" yells Heather. She tries hard to sound stern. "It's time to go home! Time to leave!"

Then she and Nathan begin handing out pieces of candy to reward kids who are willing to go. Some *pekins* come through the line more than once, giggling when Heather and Nathan catch them.

When Abu sees his soccer game is truly called, he tosses me the ball, and then helps herd the children out of the yard. Then, he hops back onto the porch, knocks on our kitchen door, and pokes his head into the room.

"I can just hold the ball for you," he says, eyeing it where it sits on the armchair. The ball is now the reddish-brown color of the earth in the yard. "I'll just hold it while I keep watch for you."

Abu's mother sells clothes several days' walk away. She won't be back until the end of the week, and the rice is gone at his house for now. He doesn't tell us this. We learn it later. Instead, he goes back outside to shoo away the kids who continue to wander into the yard. The ball rests casually between his arm and his side. He walks the length of our porch for more than an hour that evening, trying on the feeling of having his own soccer ball.

LOGIC

I am bothered by the story from Marie's grandmother.
I find L.A.

"L.A., you grew up here," I say.

"Yes, of course."

"Was there a sorcerer in your village?"

"Yes."

"Then how did you end up in medicine? How did you stop believing what the sorcerer said?"

"I went to school. I took courses in preventing disease and in healing."

"But don't people believe you? What about in your village?"

"I wanted to talk to people about prevention and healing. I was excited to do so. But people don't believe me. Here in Sierra Leone, we believe in old ways that have been tried before. Before we trust something, we want to know how old the man is who is bringing this news. I am not yet old enough to be trusted."

"Oh."

"You should talk to Stanley about this."

Stanley is a nurse, too. He is also the hospital's pharmacist. I find him in the dispensary, a great big room with white walls and a high ceiling. Long metal shelves hold neatly stacked bottles of medicine, boxes of gloves, syringes. Each section has a handwritten label stuck on the front.

"I just want to tell you," says Stanley, "that you can't tell people here that traditional medicines don't work. Sometimes when we are treating a child at the hospital, the parents will come and say that the kid has been bewitched, paid to the devil."

"Like Marie."

"Yes. But sometimes the sorcerer will have given them dried leaves to help with the bewitchment. Then the parents will say that they want the kid discharged so they can treat the bewitchment. I say to them, 'You will kill the kid if you take him out of the hospital.'

"They may leave the kid, then. But after a while, they sometimes still want him discharged. In that case, before they can take the kid, I make them sign something saying they are taking him against medical advice. Once, within only a few hours of leaving, the kid died."

"Stanley, that's terrible!"

"Yes, it is terrible."

"When do people realize that the sorcerer isn't working?"

"It's all money. They will keep paying and paying to try and fix the problem. They come to the hospital as a last resort. What we need to do — to try to do — is to get them to come immediately to the hospital."

"Are you from Kamakwie, Stanley?"

"Yes, I was born here at the hospital! My grandfather had four wives. My father was his eldest child. I was the eldest grandchild. So when I was a little boy, I had lots and lots of charms tied on me to keep me safe." Stanley laughs. He stops for a moment.

"I had those until I was seven, eight, nine years of age. Charms!" He shakes his head. "I will show you when a kid comes in with charms so you can see."

"Why did you stop believing in the charms?"

"One of my uncles sent me to school. I learned there." He pauses. "Some people believe me when I tell them the truth about medicine. But other people think I am no longer logical."

"What, that you're crazy?"

"Yes. Now that I believe in medicine, I am no longer logical!"

Stanley laughs and laughs.

GRANDMOTHER

I walk through one of the hospital wards, and notice two women sitting on one of the beds. Next to them is an empty bed frame, the mattress removed. One woman has graying hair at her temples — the only place where I can see it — the rest is wrapped under a purple-and-gold scarf. She wears beaded hoop earrings and a long necklace. Her dress is blue and yellow and red.

The other woman holds a baby boy, less than a year old. She sits straight, resting him against her left arm, which is ringed by thin, beaded bracelets. The baby wears a black amulet around his neck to help keep him safe. His head lies against her shirt, the fabric a field of daisies.

"Click, click."

They want a photograph. But they do not smile. They look at me, through my camera, beseechingly.

I bend close to show them their image on the back of my camera. The woman holding the baby starts to speak. I do not understand her language. The woman in blue and red and yellow reaches for my hand and holds it briefly.

Adama is in another part of the room. She comes over to translate for me.

"Her daughter has died."

The woman lifts the baby from the daisies up to her cheek, and keeps speaking. She looks at me instead of Adama.

"The child's mother has died. She is the grandmother. She must care for the child."

Did the mother die giving birth to the baby? I look over at the empty bed frame. *Or did she just die today? Is she why they're here? Or is one of them sick?*

A breeze blows in through the open window, carrying laughter with it; children are playing somewhere nearby. The curtains sway gently.

The woman speaks again. One sentence.

"Her daughter, the child's mother, has died," says Adama.

"I am so sorry. Please tell her, Adama, that I am so sorry to hear that."

I don't know what else to say.

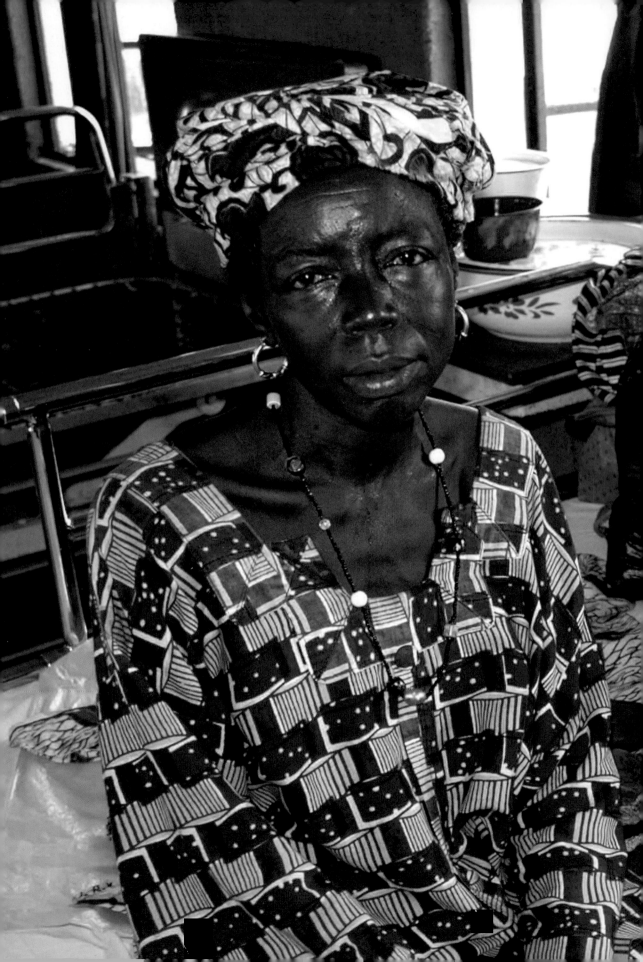

The grandmother (right)

Heather and Ya Mary Lane

QUADRUPLETS

"Hey! It's Ya Mary Lane!" Heather exclaims as we walk up a side road one day. "Ya Mary Lane is awesome!"

We round the low fence made from carefully piled cement blocks.

"Ya Mary Lane!" she calls. "*Kushe!* How are you?"

"I'm old and tired!" Ya Mary Lane laughs, leaning back in her chair. Her white hair wrinkles out from under her brown felt hat. She wears glasses and gold earrings and a cherry-red shirt. She has dimples in her cheeks. Laundry blows on a line behind her. Chickens search along the ground for food. There is a small dog.

"I see that you are back, Dr. Heather. Tell me what you are doing now."

We sit down on wooden chairs and talk for a bit. Ya Mary Lane was the only midwife in Kamakwie for years and years. She is interested in the work Heather, Jenn, and Nathan are doing in the villages.

"Education is it," she says. "This is a good thing to be doing. Some people will not listen to you. But some people will. It might help. You must try it."

At the edge of Ya Mary Lane's large yard is a short house that looks more like a garden shed. From it spill four boys under twelve. Their mother stops pounding grain in the tall mortar that stands outside the door. She watches us and gives a shy smile. Their father appears a moment later, ducking his head under the door frame as he steps out into the sun. The boys see my camera.

"Click me! Click me!"

I get up.

"You come to my house and I will cook for you," says Ya Mary Lane, holding Heather's hand in hers. "I will make you stew."

"We've got chickens from the Kakissy chief," says Heather immediately. We aren't sure what to do with the Kakissy chickens. None of us is prepared to kill them. "Can we give those for the meal?"

Ya Mary Lane grins.

"Yes, I will cook those chickens for you. Send them to me."

"We'll ask one of the *pekins* to bring them down," says Heather. Abu or Brimah is far more qualified to transport live chickens than we are. They lift them fearlessly.

A few evenings later, we sit in Ya Mary Lane's house. The wide-open door lights up the common room. The chairs have come in from the yard and circle her low table. Ya Mary Lane tells stories about her travels. She spent the war with her grown children in Italy and later California. She talks about the house she is now building in Kamakwie for orphaned children. She will take us there after dinner so we can see it. Then she and Heather, Mama J, Nathan, and Jenn start talking about medicine again.

We have just finished eating. Two boys come in to clear our dishes. A few minutes later, through the open door, I can see them sucking the remaining bits of meat off the chicken bones.

"There was one day," says Ya Mary Lane, "when a woman had quadruplets. Quadruplets! Four babies!" She slaps her knee and laughs.

"I had no idea there were four babies there! The infants just kept coming and coming so fast. I was tying off the umbilical cords as quickly as I could. I had to run for more string to do the job. I was so happy to hear all of the babies crying!"

"Did they all live?" I ask.

"Yes! They were all crying when they were born."

She is triumphant, and I love the thought of those babies seeing her wide, cheery smile at the start of their lives. I imagine her holding their wobbly bodies up in her practiced hands and kissing their cheeks.

"No, did they all survive in the end?" This time it is Nathan who asks.

A cold shadow drops over Ya Mary Lane's face.

"All but one died eventually." Her tone is even, colorless.

We had missed the point. For Ya Mary Lane, what mattered was that those four babies had lived. It was not their deaths she recorded, but the shining miracle of their lives.

Two of the boys in
Ya Mary Lane's yard

DIAMONDS

There is a small orange-and-green shop on the way up to the hospital from town, near the police office. The words *Central Diamond Office* are painted on it in yellow letters. Underneath, someone had painted cartoon pictures of diamonds. The corrugated metal roof is mostly new.

"There are not diamonds here," says Steven when I ask him about it. "The diamonds are in the east. In Kono District."

Steven knows. He worked in the diamond fields.

"The work was very tedious. Very tedious," he tells me. He closes his eyes for a minute, as if against bright sun shining on water. He rubs his forehead. His eyebrows are drawn together. We are sitting in my interview room. There is a light breeze blowing through the window. I wait.

"During the day, we worked in the diamond fields. At night, we worked in the illicit diamond fields."

"Illicit?"

"They were outside of the other fields, in places that were not approved for diamond mining. Then we would have to be careful. If police saw you, you would have to run. But everyone worked in both fields. You could work day and night for money. I was there, in the diamond area, when the war first broke out. I left from there."

He fled with his younger brothers to Makeni.

Not safe. The war came there, too.

"One day, there was a knock on my door. It was some rebels. They said they did not want to hurt me. They had their weapons behind their backs."

They moved into his house with him, and they would not let him move out.

"*Did* they hurt you?"

"No, they never hurt me. But it was difficult because they took drugs. They took drugs particularly before they were about to make an attack on a village. The drugs made them change their moods. One moment they would talk to me nicely, like I am talking to you. The next moment, they would yell at me. I never knew what they would do. I was never sure. But — I could listen to them."

Steven's eyes glint.

"They spoke to each other in Mende. I knew how to speak Mende from when I was in the east. They never found out that I understood it, so I could listen to their planning. One time they were planning to attack one of my friends. I was able to warn him to go away before they did."

Steven has a catalogue of the war in his head. It lives in his mind like a language. The war started in 1991. It was eight years before the United Nations stepped in to try and bring peace to Sierra Leone — nine years before the British troops intervened and, in a few short battles, ended the war.

Steven describes the complex series of events as though he can see them flashing slowly, one after another, on a screen in front of him.

I listen but, as he talks, I can't help thinking of him standing in the river, bending down time and again to fill his shaker with mud, searching for sparkling stones.

I learn that Steven is just a year older than I am. He is smart. That is easy to see. While he was looking for diamonds, I was finishing high school. While he was living with rebel soldiers who might have murdered him in an instant, I was in university. Safe. Oblivious.

Not fair.

Steven stops talking. We sit quietly for a moment.

"Steven, can I ask you something?" I say.

"Yes, of course."

"Not about the war."

"Yes, of course."

"Steven, what would you like to do?"

"What do you mean?"

"Well, I know you have your job as a driver for Brimah Samura."

"I have a very good job with Mr. Samura."

"I understand that. I understand that you appreciate it, and that it is a good job. But, Steven, if you could do anything you wanted, what would you do? If you could be anything."

Steven looks down at my desk. I am not sure how to read his expression. Quizzical, maybe. Or unsure. There is something in the depth of his dark eyes that is searching.

"Engineer," he says.

I smile. *Perfect.*

"I think you would make a great engineer, Steven! I know you could do it. And there is such a need for engineers here. So much rebuilding to do. So many roads and buildings."

"Yes, think about Freetown."

"Yes. I think you should try to do it."

"University is very expensive. Very expensive. I cannot pay for it."

"I see." I stop for a second. "But don't they have scholarships? Maybe you could go to the university and talk to the admissions department. They could see how much potential you have. They could help you." As I say it, my heart sinks. *Probably a long shot.*

"Maybe I will try," he says. "I must go now. Thank you." And he gets up and leaves.

Maybe I shouldn't have asked.

I rest my head on my hand and stare out the window. I wish I knew the rules here.

When I get back to the bunkhouse, Jenn and Nathan are sitting on the couch, surrounded by long balloons. The *pekins* stand in the door, watching as Nathan inflates the balloons using the hand pump he brought for the soccer ball.

"Okay," says Jenn, who is holding a book, *How to Make Balloon Animals*, "let's try one."

The kids, Jenn, and I laugh as Nathan twists the balloons, trying to follow her directions. But I'm not in the mood for balloons. I'm uneasy.

I go into my room and pull my laptop out from under my bed. I usually only use it to back up my photographs and the recordings I make of my interviews. I try to save the battery because I never know when we'll have power to charge it. But I turn it on now.

I had downloaded information on the war before I left, looking at it briefly. But now I want to make sure I have my facts straight. I want Steven to know that I care to get them right.

I read about the staggering corruption of Sierra Leone's government. As it grew richer, things like the education system, the health-care system, the justice system, completely fell apart. Just fell apart. And most people in Sierra Leone were as poor as it is possible to be. They were starving and dying. Young people, particularly, had no hope that things would ever change.

I read about how many outside groups were ready to take advantage of those young people — to use them, their anger, their despair — to get access to the wealth from Sierra Leone's diamond mines. People like Charles Taylor, the president of Liberia, the country next door, which was in the midst of its own civil war.

I read about the Sierra Leone rebel group, which Charles Taylor helped fund — the Revolutionary United Front — determined to free Sierra Leoneans from the corruption of their government.

I read about how those rebels terrorized the people in their communities.

Nothing I read explains how cruel they became. Or how cruel the government forces became. Or how it was possible they could do such unspeakable things to the people in their own communities, in their own country. Or what changed in their hearts that made them find a kind of ease in torturing others — a strange relief.

I read how both sides burned villages, massacred people, amputated their limbs. I start to read about them using children as soldiers, and I stop. Thousands of children forced to endure the worst kind of torture. I know about this already, and I cannot stand to think about it.

Diamonds, I remind myself. *Focus on the diamonds*.

Diamonds kept that war going. They funded the fighting. They funded the government troops and the rebel troops. Even groups brought in to help stop the war were concentrated on exploiting the diamonds. At one point, the government hired a South African mercenary firm to end the war. They paid them in money and in the right to mine diamonds, but the mercenaries had to get the rebels out of the mining areas first. Fewer than two hundred soldiers pushed the rebels back in a matter of weeks to get at those diamonds. The mercenaries left eventually because the Sierra Leone government couldn't afford to pay them the money it owed. But then even the first group of peacekeepers that arrived — the Nigerian ECOMOG — secretly partnered with the rebels in illegal diamond mining. The *peacekeepers*.

I close my eyes and think about Steven in the illegal diamond fields. I read about how impoverished young people, desperate for employment, worked in the dangerous riverbed mines.

Steven could not have known that the diamonds he found there were helping buy the AK-47s that would kill people in his country. The AK-47s light enough, small enough, for little children to carry.

I slam down my screen.

How many people died because of those stones?

Boys near their house in Kamakwie

SALLAY

I gather stories about the war, one after the other.

I am so curious. I remember the veterans from Remembrance Day in school. We sat cross-legged on the dusty gym floor in lopsided rows. Someone read "In Flanders Fields," and an eighth grader played the trumpet. Kids in Guides or Scouts wore uniforms, badges sewn neatly down the sleeves. The old soldiers sat in folding chairs at the front, facing us. They were usually in blue blazers with gray pants. They wore poppies and medals and sometimes hats. We gave them things. Pictures, handshakes, poetry. We learned that they gave us freedom. But we never got to *talk* to them.

I wonder what it is like to be in a war. To live a life after it.

Umaro comes to see me one day. I know his daughter, Ruth, from our yard. That Sunday she had worn a pale-yellow straw hat to church. The ribbon around the brim was translucent and frayed. She looks like her father, the angles of her jaw rising from her chin like a smile. Ruth was just born when the war began in Sierra Leone. As she grew, so did the war, wending its way from the east, down along the coast, relentless terror cutting swaths through the jungle, burning its way through the center of Sierra Leone and then north to tiny Kamakwie.

Umaro's daughter, Ruth

"There, two rebels shot my friend," says Umaro, pointing out into the yard. "I was hiding so they would not find me, too. But I saw it right in front of me. They were shooting everybody."

"Right here, outside this window?" I ask him. So close to me — separated just by time.

"Yes, next to the bush."

"And every day, every day you see that bush? You walk near that bush where this happened?"

"Yes."

He leaves, and I look at the bush. I am holding my pen. My hand starts to shake so badly that I drop it.

The stories start to come to me.

One afternoon, Steven stops me as I walk across the hospital grounds.

"I have someone for you to speak to. She is a friend of mine. You should know what happened to her in the war. You should know about these kinds of things. I have asked her, and she said she will meet you."

I wait for him the next day on our porch. We are going to walk to the interview room together. He will translate the Krio for me. But he is late. And when he arrives, he is not walking. He is driving the white truck. He sits behind the steering wheel, staring straight ahead. His dark eyes are set, determined. I can't tell if he's angry. I lean in the open window.

"My friend Sallay says she has become sick and cannot come. She has hurt her foot." His gaze does not leave the sky outside of the truck window. I wish I knew what he was thinking. "Will you go to her house?" Steven asks. He shoots the words like bullets. His gaze never leaves the sky. Then again, more softly: "Will you go into her house to talk to her there?"

"Yes, of course."

"I will go to her and tell her. Just to check that it is okay. It is important to tell these stories. I will be back." He tears off in the truck through the short grass, around the hospital, down the rutted Kamakwie road.

Within an hour, he brings me to Sallay's house. He is calm again. And in Sallay's windowless, cramped main room, he is more relaxed than he is with us. He chats in Krio with the handful of people gathered there. Then he leads me through them, behind a thin wall and into the dim bedroom.

Sallay sits on her sagging bed. Her head is hidden under a sort of low canopy. Her body is broad and she is clearly tall. I sit down next to her, bracing my legs so I will not fall into her. I worry the bed might break under our weight. Steven sits close beside us on a low chair.

Sallay does not look at me. She does not say *kushe* when I greet her. She looks briefly at Steven and then down at her hands. Then she begins to speak. Her voice is a strangled, low moan. I listen. Steven translates. He looks at Sallay tenderly.

I can see, as she speaks, that story digging into her body, clawing into her skin, twisting through her veins on its way out.

Sallay saw mothers forced by soldiers to kill their own babies.

I listen, stunned. I feel that story and its sickening details come to rest permanently in my mind. It embeds itself, tentacles like barbed wire.

She is quiet. Neither of us cries. I take her hand. Mine is cold.

"Sallay, I am so sorry. Steven," I look at him, "please tell her I am so sorry. I am so sorry, Sallay, that this happened."

She says something in Krio.

"She is sorry about the trouble about her foot," says Steven.

"I understand," I say. *Who could ever want to tell that story? Ever.*

There is a change in Sallay's face. The air, so thick and heavy while she spoke, is light. I feel her relief.

"It helps," says Steven, "for others to know. To hear."

Sallay stands up. She dwarfs the tiny room. She fills it with her grace. Her family, who have been quiet on the other side of the wall, sweep in around her, pulling her toward the door. When we go outside into that sunny day, she drapes her arm around one of her teenage sons. He says something to her, and Sallay throws back her head and laughs.

Sallay laughs with her sons

CHOICES

Mama J talks late into the night. The two of us, lying on our beds in the dark beneath our mosquito nets.

She does not know what I learned today from Sallay. I will not tell her. I cannot tell. I listen as she talks about home. She tells me about meeting her husband, Jason. We talk about our kids, about what they might be doing. Little things, like what they might be eating for supper that night.

She drifts off eventually. I cannot close my eyes.

I think of Aidan and Kate as babies. I knew from the moment Aidan opened his eyes that he was wise — gentle. Kate never slept for long. She wanted to be up, part of things. She smiled every time she caught your eye. We didn't know someone could smile so much until we met her.

What would it take — I have to ask myself — what would it take for me to kill one of them? I would never do it.

I would never do it.

How could I go on living if I did? What would I tell Mike? How could I look at him again if I killed one of our children? How could he love me?

I would be killed myself instead. Without question.

I am not like those mothers.

But I have heard too many stories now. I have heard too much.

What would you do, my mind whispers insistently, *what would you do if you knew that your life was not a substitute for the baby's?*

They would kill you and also the baby. And then all of your children. But they would torture the children first. Rape your little girls. Maybe pick one of your sons to kill his brothers and sisters himself.

If you don't kill your baby, these things will happen. If you kill your baby, they won't. Simple.

In my mind, I can see the glittering eyes. The flashing teeth. The guns in their arms. The brown dirt. I can hear, clearly, the anguished cries of my sisters here. They fill my ears.

How could this have happened in this world? How is it possible?

I cannot move. I am sure I will never sleep again.

LIST

I curl up in a chair in the common room with piles of papers from Kakissy School. They are thick and dusty from the school ground. Nathan and Jenn are making balloon animals again for the kids outside on the porch. Every now and again I can hear kids rustling near my window. If I look up suddenly, I catch them staring in at me. Then they run, laughing, down the porch stairs into the yard.

Things We Like to Do: Balance Ball is the title of the first paper.

I have seen Abu and his friends playing balance ball outside. It is sort of like dodge ball, but harder.

> *Balance ball is a game that three people play,* the article says. *One will stand on one side, and one should stand on the other end. Then one is in the middle. You use a ball and slippers to play this game. The slippers have to be in a pile in the middle. The ones on either side should try to stone the person in the middle with the ball. That person in the middle is trying to unpack the slippers in a row without being hurt by the ball. If he or she is hit by the ball, he or she loses the game. But if she has unpacked the slippers without being touched by the ball, he or she has won the game.*

The next one is *Things We Like to Do: Our Church.*

> *Our church is the WCSL Wesleyan Church of Sierra Leone Kakissy. It is located along the Kamakwie road on the ending of the village. We do services at any time. We sing songs and dance.*

There are articles about the school itself:

> *Our school is located along the Kamakwie road, 20 yards from the road. We are 140 students in school, both boys and girls. We have three classes and four teachers and the teachers speak different language groups: Temne and Limba. Also, we the students speak different language groups.*
>
> *Our school is a community school and we the students use our home clothes to attend school. We do not have uniforms to wear at school. The clothes we wear in town are the kind we use in school also.*

There are maps, all of which clearly mark the river the village uses for water. The Storytelling kids have written about rats and snakes and lions and getting palm wine from palm trees. And there are drawings of all kinds. On the back of one that shows the school with its missing walls is this list written by a girl called Sallay K:

We want school.
We want uniforms.
We want to eat in the school.
We all need books.
We need food to grow.
We need food for energy.
We need pens.
We need food.
We need supplies.

With the permission of the chief and with the help of the elders, Heather organizes a community meeting in Kakissy. She wants to make the announcement about the money to fix the school. When the benches in the big clearing beneath the trees are full, people stand. For once, kids do not play around the outside of the circle, but lean in close to hear what Heather has to say. Saidu, dressed in a shirt and tie, translates for her.

"Students at the secondary school near my home have raised money to help finish building your school here in Kakissy. I have brought that money to you." Heather sounds official at first. But then, as people began to smile around her, she can't contain herself.

"It's going to be awesome! The whole school is going to be fixed. The whole school! There should be some money left over for supplies and books for the teachers."

The chief and the elders speak, and Heather spends the rest of her time in Kakissy shaking hands with what seems like every member of the village.

I hope that Sallay K is there, amongst the girls squatting on the inner edges of the circle. I know that Heather raised the money months ago. But I still hope Sallay K believes that somehow she helped.

Kids at Kakissy
wait for Heather's
announcement

"Hey, Abu!" I call as I climb up onto the porch. He is waiting for Nathan to grab the soccer ball from inside. "How was your day at school?"

Abu loves school. I remember the day he listed off his subjects. Arabic was one of them.

"You study Arabic? Do you like it?" I could hear myself moaning about conjugating French verbs.

"Arabic? I love it!" He stretched out the word "love." His eyes sparkled.

But he wasn't smiling today.

"Today I was flogged," he says.

"You were what? Flogged? Someone hit you? Who did that?"

"At the school. I did not have my school fees, so they had to flog me."

"They hit you because you cannot pay?"

"Yes, of course."

"Where is your mother, Abu?"

Abu had brought his mother to meet us one day. She stood quietly next to him. She carried her grandson, Abu's nephew, on her back, wrapped safely in a brilliant orange-and-yellow cloth.

"Thank you," she had said in English, holding each of our hands in hers.

Abu is the kind of person who knows, just knows, that the world holds something special for him. His mother seemed tired, like she used all of her energy to keep Abu's smile in place.

"My mother is away today," Abu says.

Nathan opens the front door and tosses Abu the ball.

"Here is this guy," says Abu. He points toward the quiet friend with whom I often see him.

"What is your name?" I ask.

The boy looks at the ground. He seems concerned. Like Steven.

"I am Alusine."

"It's nice to meet you, Alusine."

He meets my eyes only briefly. Abu slings his arm around Alusine's shoulders.

"This is my brother. He is my friend, but he is my brother. When I have no food, he feeds me. His family feeds me."

Alusine grabs the ball from Abu and tosses it down to the ground.

Abu grins and jumps off the porch.

Abu (left) and Alusine

FIRE ANTS

"You'll never see someone take their pants off faster," says Dr. Emmett as he pauses by our porch on one of his afternoon walks. "Those are fire ants."

The ants march perpetually across our yard, tumbling over stones and under the dried leaves curling on the ground. They form a thick black line that dips and swerves like waves in a child's drawing.

I can tell you that Dr. Emmett is right.

I can tell you that if you stand accidentally in their way and are wearing flip-flops, hundreds of fire ants can travel three-and-a-half feet up your bare leg in a matter of seconds, biting and stinging the whole way.

I can tell you that once you have ripped off your skirt in an attempt to get rid of the ants, you will find them lodged in your belly button.

And, I can tell you that your legs will be, for days afterward, a mass of painful bites.

I don't remember if Nathan was bitten or if he was just tired of watching it happen to the rest of us.

"You must burn the ants," the kids tell us. "That is the only way to do it."

So Nathan marches outside with a can of the fuel we use for our stove. He pours it over the line of ants and lights them on fire.

And that is that.

Nathan takes on the fire ants.
Heather directs.

SON

"You want me to take him?"

Dr. Heather steps out onto the porch. The yard is unusually quiet. Or perhaps it just feels that way.

The mother nods. The boy is probably twelve or thirteen. His shirt is tucked carefully into his pants. His father stands close beside him.

"You take him for your son. You can take him back to your country."

"No, I can't do that," says Heather. Her voice is immediately soft, compassionate.

The mother pushes the boy forward.

"You can take him for your son."

"No, I can't do that. He belongs here. He belongs here with you."

The mother breathes out heavily. After a few seconds, she nods.

The family walks back along the length of the porch, down the steep concrete stairs, through the yard.

A tangle of emotions hangs behind them. Hope. Pride. Sadness. Disappointment. Love.

What conversations must have taken place amongst the elders in that boy's family: Should they ask? Which child should they choose to go? Who should have the chance?

Maybe he is the eldest. Or the smartest. Or the one who works the hardest.

The doctor would see how special he was. The doctor would see how handsome. The doctor would see what a good son he would be for her. The doctor would take him. The doctor would send him to school. The doctor would give him a life like hers. He would be rich.

That boy, from North America, would be able to help them all.

Despite the sweetness of the dream, that mother had to force herself to push her boy closer to Dr. Heather. I could see her brain ordering her arm to do the opposite of what it wanted. She was not to pull him, beloved child, close to her. She was to push him away to a world of opportunity so different from theirs in Kamakwie. She was to push him forward.

SOKO

"You need to talk to this guy to hear what happened to him in the war," L.A. says to me one day. "You will see what happened when we could not trust each other any longer. We could not be kind to kids or women whom we did not know without consequences. Can we drive in your truck?"

Steven picks us up. We drive out of Kamakwie for a long while. We are going, L.A. tells me, to a village called Kamalenka. I like the way it sounds when he says it, the syllables racing on their way out: Ka-ma-len-ka.

The dirt road chases shafts of afternoon sunlight through dense trees, tall grasses, and open fields. Now and then people walk along the side of it, some pushing bicycles, most balancing loads on their heads.

L.A. says something to Steven in Krio, points off to the left, and Steven turns abruptly from the road onto a field. Nothing marks the place that I can see. I sit up straight, suddenly uneasy. Where are they taking me?

"L.A., I don't see the road," I say. "What happened to the road?"

"There is no road."

"We usually drive on roads to places in North America."

"Ah!"

We keep driving.

"Um . . . how did you know where to turn?"

"I just know the way." He laughs. Steven laughs, too. We drive through the unmarked grass. A few moments later we see people walking again, waving this time as we pass.

"This guy we are going to meet is called Soko," says L.A.

We drive slowly into Kamalenka. Children run after our truck in a long line, swerving behind us like the tail of a kite.

The village is beautiful and filled with trees. Their leaves scatter the sunlight in shifting patterns across the ground. Houses arc along the village road. Some are round, some square, all topped with tall, pointed roofs of prickly grass. Small peppers are spread out in front of the houses and on large concrete pads to dry in the sun like vivid red artwork in patterns of squares, rectangles, circles.

Peppers dry on the ground near the blue-and-yellow church

Soko meets us in the doorway of the Kamalenka Wesleyan Church. He is tall and muscular like a tree, one arm sawed off partway down; his shirtsleeve hangs limp below it.

The church is a large rectangular building. Although the door is open, the blue wooden shutters are closed over the windows. The room settles into a gentle darkness. We sit in the first two rows of pews. L.A. is translating the Krio for me. He is still in his white lab coat from the hospital. The blue top of a pen peeks out of his pocket.

Soko's arm had to be cut off at the Kamakwie hospital after he was captured and tortured by the ECOMOG peacekeepers.

"The peacekeepers," I say. My arms and chest feel heavy.

"Yeees," says L.A., stretching out the word, his voice rising at the end. "It was the government peacekeepers sent by West Africa to help end the war. The ECOMOG."

I look at Soko. He sits in complete stillness. He speaks quietly.

"He was working on the farm outside of the village," translates L.A. "A woman came running from another chiefdom and begged him to help her. She was escaping the rebels who were coming to her village. She wanted to secure a place in this village before others who were also escaping arrived and there was no room left.

"Soko wanted to help her. His wife was on the farm with him. She told him not to help that lady. She told him that she did not trust her. She was sure that lady was a spy for the rebels."

Soko stops speaking. He had been looking at the ground as he talked. He looks up at L.A. now and speaks directly to him.

"He thought that this woman was honest. He thought that this woman needed his help. How could he ignore her? Why could she not stay with them? So he left the farm and brought her to the elders in his village.

"'Please be in charge of this lady,' he asked them. 'I want to go back to my farm.'

"There was another woman in the village who was also afraid the lady was a rebel come to spy on them. She went to the peacekeepers. She told the ECOMOG that Soko was housing a rebel. The peacekeepers lay in wait. When Soko came back from his farm, they ambushed him."

Big, strong Soko, felled.

"'What did I do?' he asked them.

"'We are going to know what it is you have done!' they said to him.

"They would not let him explain. They would not let him tell them why he was helping that woman.

"They captured him and put him in the church."

"They put him in a church, L.A.? Was it this one?"

"Yes. This is the church.

"They broke his arm. They tied him up. He begged not to be tied up. He begged not to because of his broken-up arm. The pain. And he must protect it. He needs it to work in the fields. He needs it to heal properly. He promised he would just follow them wherever they wanted him to go. But they tied him anyway and left him here. Then they went and found two of his family members — two uncles. They pulled them out from their houses and they shot them."

I close my eyes against the image.

"They killed the uncles because they were related to Soko. Then they brought Soko to the top of the hill where their commander had a house. They threw him from the window of that house down the hill. Then they left him. After a while, they threw him in the back of a Land Rover like a bag of rice."

"Did anyone help him? His friends?"

"What could they do? What could they do? They would be killed! They tried to follow when the ECOMOG drove away with Soko in the back. They started to follow after the truck, but the soldiers fired their weapons — warning shots. What could they have done? They would be killed."

Soko, folded into the back of the peacekeeping truck, curving down his village road, shooting pain from his broken arm. His uncles murdered. His friends able to offer him only the gesture of running after the truck.

"Fortunately for him, the peacekeepers took him to the section chief in Kamakwie. His character was known to this chief.

Soko in the door of the church

"'What have you done?' asked the chief.

"'I do not know what I have done,' Soko told him.

"'Do you know of this man?' the ECOMOG asked the chief.

"'Yes.'

"'Unbind him, then.'

"So they did. By then it was too late for the arm. His arm had to be cut off at the hospital. It had died."

I look toward the bright doorway. We had been alone to start, the three of us and this story. But people from the village fill the pews behind us now. They had filed in as Soko spoke, silent witnesses.

"Look at how strong and big he is," says L.A. "Even so, with only one hand, he cannot work on the farm any longer. He can no longer help. He has six children."

"How does he survive?"

"By the grace of God."

"What happened to the woman he tried to help? Was she a rebel spy?"

L.A. shrugs.

"L.A., he still lives in the village where this happened to him. Are the people who accused him of helping the rebels — is that woman who went to the ECOMOG — still here?"

"Yes, of course."

"But L.A., this is a tiny village. He must see her." I look from L.A. to Soko. "Soko, you must see her."

"Yes, of course."

Soko's eyes are bloodshot. Tired. He lifts his amputated arm a little.

"At first, when he thought of it, he wanted to retaliate by stabbing the lady," translates L.A. "But it is our responsibility to forgive. He was already handicapped. Nothing could be changed with his anger. So then when he walked by her, he just said, 'Hello.' Just, 'Hello.'"

Soko stands up. He walks to the front of the church and unbuttons his shirt. He takes it off. He wants me to photograph him, to record part of what he has lost.

THE FIELD

We are quiet in the truck when we leave Kamalenka. As we drive out, the village looks different to me. It is as if the memory of the war has a presence of its own — as if it sits like a soft charcoal outline at the edges of everything.

I can see now how dangerous those pretty grass roofs are. How quickly those roofs would burn, how easily flames would hop from one to the other.

I can see now how peppers spread in patterns are signs of peace — of undisturbed space, of hearts light enough to create something lovely.

Steven crests the hill that starts our unmarked road through the fields, and suddenly there is a tower of thick smoke, gray, white, black, pouring ahead of us. There is fire, hot, raging.

And then the sound of children yelling.

I panic.

"L.A., the field is on fire!"

"Yes, it is on fire."

He is undisturbed. Steven slows down.

As we get closer, I see children racing through the field, smoke rising from their bare feet. They are cheering and jumping, arms thrown high in the air. Then two teenagers come beside us, pushing a giant boulder over the burning ground.

"L.A., what are they doing? Those kids are going to get hurt! They're going to be burned!"

"They're making a field for football."

"What?"

"They're flattening a field for football. Someone has given them that field for it."

I watch, fascinated. Kids wave to us as they tear over the ground. When they see my camera perched on the edge of my open window, some turn around, yelling, "Click me! Click me!"

"Um . . . L.A.? Isn't it a little dangerous?"

"Dangerous? Why? It is not yet really the dry season. It would be dangerous to have the fire in the dry season."

"Ah. Of course." I pull my camera reluctantly in the window. I am worried it will melt.

We drive away through the smoke, the kids' happy cries drifting skyward behind us.

Flattening the field

Girls in their WCSL
school uniforms

WCSL

On one of my first days in Kamakwie, I took a photograph of a group of kids outside of the hospital. They had just come from school, wandering over the top of the hill, chattering together. There are twenty-five of them crowded into the picture. Twenty of the children are dressed in school uniforms. Five are not.

You cannot go to school in Kamakwie unless you can pay — not just for the school fees, but also for a uniform. I think of those five kids meeting up with the others at the end of the day. It is difficult to get ahead in Kamakwie from what I see. Impossible, in many ways, without school.

Most of the children in the photograph are wearing the green-and-yellow uniforms from WCSL school, where Sainy teaches. The five of us take the picture books there one day to read to the kids. I take my extra paper, too. If there are pens, I will ask the older students to write letters to kids their age in North America. I wonder what they will say.

It is chilly early that morning. I hadn't expected cold weather in Sierra Leone, so have only a thin sweater with me. I pull it around my shoulders and shiver as we walk down past houses, around gardens, the sound of shortwave radios meeting us now and again. We come upon a clearing after a few minutes. A family is sitting next to a smoldering fire, lit, as cooking fires are, from long pieces of wood splayed between three large rocks. They are not eating, though there are two wide plastic bowls full of biscuits. Perhaps they are to sell. The children watch us. One little boy in shorts and an open shirt holds his arms tightly across his bare chest, as though trying to keep warm. In the middle of the group sits their beautiful grandmother. Pink-orange sunlight cuts through the trees, lighting her face.

We gather students on our walk. Some we know from our porch. White Boy and City Boy jump out from behind a bush, squealing delightedly at Dr. Heather. Brimah stays close to Mama J.

WCSL is completely different from Kakissy school. It is a collection of three buildings, each about the size of the whole of Kakissy school. There are seven classes at WCSL as well as a preschool — 813 students altogether: 452 boys and 361 girls. The main building is a deep yellow. In some places, kids have scratched words on it with chalk or the edges of rock. We round the corner and there, leaning against the wall closest to the back of the building, is Abu Kamara, one arm behind his back. In the other he holds his worn exercise book. He does not see me. He looks intently, instead, at the schoolyard.

Kids are pouring in from all angles. Some hold slates in their hands — tiny chalkboards rimmed in bright-colored plastic. Many have short brooms made of stiff grass. Others have big rocks balanced on their palms — I assume samples for a school project. I see a little girl carrying a chair on her head for a teacher. Almost all of the children hold black plastic bags like the one Isotu was so anxious to have back from us.

The students clean the schoolyard when they arrive. They sweep it with their brooms and pick up fallen leaves in bunches, tucking them into their black bags. By the time the older kids begin to call them into their lines, that schoolyard looks as though it has been vacuumed.

We talk with Mr. Bangura, the headmaster, as the students file into their classrooms. Within seconds I can see little faces peering out of the open windows. First, just a few pop up, look at us, and then disappear in a fit of laughter. Then, shortly, the windows are packed full, the kindergarten children leaning out to wave. Each of us takes books to a different class. I go to Class Six, where the oldest kids are. They have one building to themselves. The classroom is made of painted concrete blocks. The ceiling is corrugated metal. There are no lights, only sections of the wall that use blocks cut in a diamond pattern; bits of sunshine work through their centers. The students sit at wooden benches behind long narrow tables. At the front of the room is a cracked and worn chalkboard.

"How many students are in your class?" I ask the teacher.

"146 students," he says.

"You are the only teacher for all of these kids?"

"Oh, yes."

"How old are they?"

"It depends. Sometimes they are twelve, sometimes as old as eighteen."

"That old?"

"Some terms, they can pay the fees. Some, they cannot. For this reason, it can take students many years to finish primary school."

The students have pens and exercise books like the one Abu Kamara holds. But they learn mainly by repeating information back to their teacher.

We pass out the paper I brought. The kids set immediately to work writing, whispering to one another. I read the letters later that night by the light of my headlamp.

Dear Friend, begins one.

> *I am happy to write you this letter about a friend. I am a school boy. I am in Class Six. My father and mother are dead. Only my aunt is taking care for me. I wanted to attend the Secondary School, but my aunt is a poor woman. I only pay my school fees when I work in the farm. I work potatoes, cassava, pepper, and some corn seeds. I am twelve years of age. We have two seasons in Sierra Leone. These are the dry season and the wet or rainy season. The capital city of Sierra Leone is Freetown. The wet season is from May to October and the dry season is from November to April. I am black in color. I hope you are glad for this letter. I greet you in the name of God. Thank you sir or ma.*

Dear Friend, begins the next.

> *I am here by writing you this letter just to help me for my school problem because I do not have a father and mother. The war killed them. I will tell you to let you help me for the problems in my body. I will not have food in my house.*
>
> *I want to learn but I do not have parents to pay my school fees. Please, supply me with two bags of rice and the money for my school fees. Thank you my friend.*

And then,

> *I write this letter to my Friend. My mother is a farmer and my father is a farmer and my grandmother is a farmer. We go to the farm and work. I would like you to be my friend. I am happy to write this to you. I write*

Class Six

this letter for you to send me a bike. I live in Kathimbo, and it is four miles from here to Kamakwie to walk by foot to come to school. It hurts my feet.

My father was a farmer, but he is dead, says another. *My mother was a farmer, but she is dead now. My grandmother, she is an old woman. I go in the bush and find wood to sell so we can eat food in the house. The people cannot give my grandmother food. My friend, you go and send for me a bicycle, a bag, books, pens, and sandals. Thank you.*

And,

I am very happy to write you this letter. Please help me for school materials. The thing I want you to help me with is school shoes and a uniform. My father is a farmer and he likes to work in the rainy season because he wants his children to go to school. My father lives in a village. He is a very old man and he has five children and he wants them to go to school because he never went to school. My father tries very hard to send all of the children to school, but we do not have money for all of the children. Please friend, do it for me.

Letter after letter after letter talks about school fees, about having to farm to earn the money to go to school, about parents who have died. The weight of their troubles pours through their attempts to write a "proper" letter:

How is the weather in North America? The subjects I like are English and mathematics. Moreover, the games that I like best are playing football and volleyball.

The papers fall onto my bed. I sit, rocking slowly back and forth, my arms wrapped around my knees. The need, the suffering, are shattering.

I pick up one more.

I know that you will help some of us in our school, writes Kabba K. *Every year I am promoted to another class. But I don't have a person to take care of my school fees. I like white people because they help children to be educated. Any stranger who comes to our school to visit, we like that person. I send greetings to all of you white people.*

SCHOOL FEES

Mama J and Heather have settled school fees with Mr. Bangura. It costs five dollars to send each child to primary school for the whole year. Thirty dollars for secondary school.

Five dollars. I kept Abu Kamara wondering for the sake of five dollars.

I had assumed it was a lot more. So many children couldn't go. Why hadn't I just asked?

I want to see Mr. Bangura.

I have loved Mr. Bangura since the afternoon he came to my interview room to talk to me about the war.

"The rebel soldiers found me at my house," he told me. "And straight away they went to my goat pen. They took all my goats for their food. They even took my pregnant goat. I said to them, 'Please, gentlemen. Leave this she-goat.'"

They would not.

"I am not a military man," Mr. Bangura had said. "I am a poor schoolteacher. Let us at least be kind to animals." And then something broke in him. "If you want to come kill *me*," he said, "then you can have my she-goat."

"For this goat you want to die?" the soldiers asked. "We are going to shoot you directly in your stomach."

"Okay," said Mr. Bangura.

"J.A.! J.A.!" his wife pleaded. "Leave these people! They are very bloody! They will destroy your life!"

"No!" said Mr. Bangura. "I will go with my goat." And he followed the soldiers and his she-goat to the WCSL schoolyard.

"The soldiers drew a line on the ground. A line of demarcation. They said to me that if I dared cross the line, I would lose my life. 'The birds of the air will eat your flesh,' they said. I said, 'Okay,' and then walked across the line toward my goat."

The soldiers killed his goat.

Mr. Bangura wept.

"We could not, at that time, even be kind to a pregnant animal," he said. I looked at him in the silence that followed. Dignified. Brave. Compassionate.

This morning, I find Mr. Bangura in the school office. He shows me the benches he is fixing with some of the money we gave to the school. They are stacked against the wall, new wood bright against the old.

"Mr. Bangura, what do you know about Abu Kamara?" I ask. "What kind of boy is he?"

"Abu Kamara? He is a very nice boy."

"He asked me to pay his fees."

"Yes, they are paid."

"Would you give him this money to buy a uniform?" I pass leones to Mr. Bangura.

"Yes, of course." Mr. Bangura looks at me kindly. "Abu Kamara is a nice, nice boy, Kathleen. He is a smart boy." He is quiet for a few seconds.

And then, "You will find him by the school wall most mornings. He is by the wall. Isotu is by the trees."

"What does she do there?"

"She weeps. She weeps while she watches the other children line up."

Abu Kamara (right) against the school wall

WHITE BOY

On our last Sunday afternoon, Jenn and I go for a walk. We see White Boy. He is lying across the concrete wall that separates one side of his front porch from the other. He wears cut-off jean shorts and a dusty white T-shirt.

Laundry hangs on the porch — long pieces of fabric: purple, green, red, yellow. Little girls' dresses.

There are four kids on the porch with him — two boys, and two girls. All are older than he is, except for the smallest girl. She might be three years old. The oldest boy — maybe twelve — holds her. She bends over, pretending to try and escape his arms, giggling.

In the midst of it, White Boy is just hanging out. Thinking. Watching the people passing by.

White Boy

Maria

CHILD SOLDIERS

I start taking naps during the day, hoping that the light will keep the bad dreams away.

Today it does not work.

I dream of a North American school. There is a white drinking fountain next to hooks filled with raincoats and bright backpacks. The letters of the alphabet are posted above the board. There are children, heads bent over their desks, coloring with fresh crayons. I can see the new packages lying open in front of them.

Then it switches. I am outside, red-brown dirt scattered with crisp mango leaves under my feet. I stand next to children who are crushing infants with stones.

That's when I wake up.

"Yes, they took kids from here," L.A. had said when I asked him if there were child soldiers from Kamakwie.

"Are they back now?"

"Some of them are here. But most of them died. Because they were not militarily trained, most of them died."

The rebel troops and the government troops — both sides in the war — took young people and used them as soldiers. Teenagers. Little kids. About half of the child soldiers in Sierra Leone were under fourteen. Some were just five. The little ones were the bravest. They would put them at the front of battles. Those sweet *pekins* did not know to be afraid of dying.

The child soldiers were forced to fight. To kill. Sometimes their own families. To spy on their neighbors, to light villages on fire, to steal, to cut off people's hands with dull machetes. The girl soldiers were raped and raped.

It haunts me. I dream about children looking for their mothers. Asking me to please find their mothers. They are clutching guns. They know their mothers will take the guns. I have no idea where the mothers are. I try to take the guns but can't.

Sometimes, when I am sitting on the blue bench on our porch, watching the kids playing soccer or balance ball, I start to worry that they are not safe. That if it happened again, they would be taken, too. Abu. Alusine. Binty. Maria. Isotu. White Boy. Gentle Brimah.

I imagine them crouching with their AK-47s in the tall grass, waiting, desperately still. I imagine them frightened and in pain when their commanders cut them with knives, packing the wound with cocaine so that they would act fearlessly. I imagine them missing their parents and sisters and brothers. I imagine them walking and walking and walking, not allowed to slow down or stop when they are tired. I imagine them learning not to cry in the night when they are scared or sad because the children who do are shot dead. I imagine them longing for the familiar patch of stars through their window at home, for a kindly moon following them after dark.

TRUTH

We knew.

The words cut through my sleep like an angry razor blade.

I lie stiff in my bed, blood icing my veins.

The international community — people in the First World — North Americans — our governments — people who could *do* something — knew what the soldiers were doing to the children of Sierra Leone.

We also knew that the soldiers were killing with abandon.

We knew that they were hacking off people's hands, noses, feet, genitals.

We knew that they were locking people in their houses and lighting them on fire, listening to them burn to death.

We knew that the mercenaries pushed back the rebels in a matter of weeks. We knew they did it for profits from the diamond mines.

I had been thinking about the *diamonds*. How could people buy diamonds when they knew they were financing a war?

Fewer than 200 soldiers pushed back the rebels *in a matter of weeks*.

We knew how little of our military force it would take to stop the war.

And we waited.

Merciful God.

Janet sleeps soundly.

I cry until I think I cannot breathe.

WAR

I am desperate to find this boy's mother.

"Heather, please, send word," I say. "She knows you from your last trip. She doesn't know me. She'll come if you ask for her."

When the mother arrives, it is growing dark. She sits in our common room and chats with Heather. I wait, anxiously, for the conversation to slow. Heather introduces us.

"Kathleen is writing a book."

Then Heather leaves the room. We are alone.

"I talked to your son, today," I say. My voice is shaking. "I asked him if he remembered the war."

She tilts her head slightly. Her brown eyes are flecked with amber and seem bottomless as she fixes them on me.

"I am so sorry," I say. "I had no idea."

For all of my reading, for all of my listening, what do I know about war?

"What was it like?" I had asked him — a sixteen-year-old, tall, with a square jaw, and a space between his front teeth.

"I will tell you," he said.

He is six years old and living in Freetown with his father and mother and little brother. They are there together when the rebel forces launch the attack they call "Operation No Living Thing." The soldiers walk through the streets, shooting, beating, burning. Bodies fall on top of the corpses already rotting along the roads, white bones poking through flaking black skin.

His mother is pregnant. She takes him and his brother to the river to wash. His father comes running. His eyes are wild. The rebels are coming close. They will be killed. There is no time to go home for clothes, shoes. No time to get anything. They have to go *now*. He runs as fast as he can run. His brother is crying. He can hear his parents' ragged breath.

People are being shot. The guns hurt his ears. They race into an empty house. They hide.

Not safe. Not a dream. The rebels come. There are so many of them. Tall. Angry. Loud. They drag them from the house.

"You are pregnant! Is it a boy baby or a girl baby?" A soldier pulls out his big knife. "We can find out."

His mother is trying to convince them. She is not pregnant, she says. Not pregnant. It is just her clothing. The soldiers grab his father.

"Papa! Papa! Mama! Papa!" the boy cries.

Then his mother is weeping, pleading with the rebels not to kill their father. Crying at their feet. Begging them in the name of Allah, God, Jesus Christ. Spare his life! Don't kill this good man! Not in front of his children!

And then his father disappears.

"Maybe he has gone to California." Tears course down his cheeks. "We are waiting for him to come home to us. He will come."

Oh, my love. I think they killed them all.

I wished that he were small enough to pick up and rock on my lap. I wished I could make it go away. I had no idea that such a story terrorized him while he sang and played football near our porch.

"I had no idea," I say to his mother again. "I did not know what had happened. I would never have asked him if I did."

I am crying now. I cannot stop. I cannot erase what he saw, heard, smelled, felt. All of these children around me. What they saw, heard, smelled, felt. I cannot give them back what they lost.

"Yes, it is painful to remember," she says. Her voice is calm. "But when you share the problems, you ease them. You will help ease them. You may tell this story, but you should not tell our names. The story is enough."

She is quiet. She takes my hands.

"I will tell you this story again," she says. "He was only a child. This is an adult story." She whispers it to me in the darkness.

The little boy she was pregnant with lived, but died when he was four.

"You must be so angry," I say. "You must hate the rebels so much."

She tightens her grip on my hands. She looks me straight in the eyes. She no longer whispers. Her voice is clear and firm.

"How can I want hatred in my heart? In the hearts of my children? So this can happen again? After what we have been through, how can I want their hearts filled with anything but the love of God? We need peace!"

LEAVING

It was as though Isotu had been dead before. That's what I think when I see her after she learns that her school fees are paid. She is transformed. Her whole self is alight. Her eyes sparkle. She simply can't stop smiling. She has come back to life.

It is our final day in Kamakwie.

I spend part of it with Mohammed and Marie.

"Goodbye, wonderful boy!" I say to Mohammed, holding him in the air. He smiles, of course. "Be safe."

Marie can sit up now. Someone has wrapped her head in a tangerine scarf. It has pink-and-white suns on it.

I kiss her cheek. "I love you, sweet girl," I whisper into her ear.

Marie never once spoke to me. Her eyes told me different stories than Mohammed's. I watch them carefully now. They still say they are tired.

And then I wander back to our place where Mama J is waiting with beaming Isotu. We are going to town to buy Isotu the uniform she needs for school. I can't wait. We are going to surprise her with a Sunday dress, too, and shoes.

Heather and Nath had gone earlier that day to take Abu school shopping. His fees are paid, but he needs clothes.

"We went a little crazy," says Nathan. "But come on! He had none of the things we asked him about — shoes, belts, extra pants. He was so excited about everything. It was great."

"Maybe we shouldn't have bought so much," says Heather. "But he's just such a great kid!"

Jenn sits on the porch, reading to the kids waiting there. I try not to think of how few of them have what we are giving Isotu, what Abu has received.

We have a porch full of people that night. The kids come first. They play football and balance ball and they crowd onto the blue bench. I can see Isotu squished in amongst them, laughing. White Boy and City Boy dangle their legs over the side of the porch. Some kids lean against the

Isotu

Goodbyes

yellow concrete walls and the porch poles, reading alone or to one another. The books I brought are going the next morning to Mr. Bangura for the school, along with the ball. Heather and Jenn and Mama J and Nathan hand out the rest of the candy and little prizes.

It becomes dark too soon, I think, as the children begin to leave for home, clasping their toys and chewing their gum. Too soon, I think, as the noise quiets and the bench holds only Brimah and Binty and Maria and Isotu.

And then, out of the darkness, comes Abu Kamara. This time he is not alone. He has two friends, maybe brothers, with him. He has heard from Mr. Bangura about his school fees and new uniform. He smiles and shakes my hand.

"Work hard. Study hard." As I say it, I realize how silly it is. Of course he will.

And then he is gone.

I begin to feel lonesome for Kamakwie. I go back inside, where the table, once piled with crayons and pencils and presents, is clean.

Abu knocks at my door. As always, Alusine is beside him. They step inside.

"I would like a watch," says Abu, pointing to his wrist.

"Abu, you have gotten a lot of things today. You have to stop asking for more." I am irritated.

Abu says nothing, but his intelligent brown eyes meet mine. He is not smiling.

What I would give for that moment back. When have I not wanted more, too?

We will leave in the early morning, and with us will go Abu's sense of limitless possibility. Why had I not let him enjoy even the thought of it for a few extra hours — a teenager who has worried for his lifetime about having food to eat, whose future is strangled by poverty?

Because I don't think of Abu that way.

I think of him like he thinks of himself. Special. Someone the world waits for.

Abu turns abruptly and points to Alusine, the quiet. Alusine looks at the floor, the familiar concerned look on his face.

"He has something to say," says Abu.

"What is it, Alusine?"

He will not look up. There is an uncomfortable silence.

"What is it, Alusine? What's wrong?"

"My mother has no money for shoes." His voice is low and tense. "Our mother is getting tired."

Abu smiles at him encouragingly, and then looks up at me.

I had not thought to offer anything to Alusine. I didn't understand, until then, that Alusine's family shares with hungry Abu not because there is extra food, but because there is food at all.

Abu takes the money from me and slips it into Alusine's pocket. Alusine keeps looking at the ground, his brow furrowed.

I try to say something funny to make the boys laugh. I tell them about going home to snow and show them pictures of it on my computer, my kids bundled up in snow pants and hats and mitts. I can hear Brimah starting to play the drum outside. We hurry out. I know that while I was talking to Abu and Alusine, Heather told Brimah he could have her drum to keep.

Adults had come to the porch by then. Umaro sits on the bench with his guitar. There is L.A. and Adama and some teachers from the high school. And there is wonderful Sainy. People are coming to say goodbye.

Sainy pulls me aside. "Do not forget about Sierra Leone," he says, smiling. "Sometimes we worry that we will be forgotten now that the war is over."

"We will pray that all of you will come back," says Reverend Alusine, who has arrived on his motorbike. He looks at me and grins, calling out softly, "Com-mu-ni-ty!"

There is singing and dancing — all of us on the porch under the starry sky. And there is Brimah, sitting next to the adults, drumming his heart out. He is so good that for a few moments his elders stop their music to let him play alone. His hands blur. He cannot help but smile.

And then, eyes closed, he begins to sing, "Tell him *thankee*, tell him, tell Papa God *thankee*."

Steven near the airport

NEXT

In the Sierra Leone Truth and Reconciliation Commission's final report on the war I read: *The Commission laments the fact that the international community declined to intervene in the unfolding human catastrophe in Sierra Leone until at a very late stage.*

We knew what was happening, and we declined to intervene. Until a very late stage.

As though it were a dinner invitation.

They needed us, and we didn't help.

Sometimes I think I will drown in the sorrow of it, that I will get lost in my rage.

We are by the sea now. At a hotel near the airport. Going home. I stand by a brick wall and watch tomato-colored sails waving over long, narrow boats. In the distance, walking toward me, are Nathan and Steven. They are laughing. Steven's arms sway at his sides; he smiles easily.

I think about what I have heard. About what I have seen.

I think about the man sitting near the Primary Chief. I think about the mothers who lost their babies. I think about the gifts from the people in Kakissy. I think about Abu and Brimah and Binty and Maria. Faces begin to slip in front of me. Mohammed, White Boy, Alusine, Sallay, Soko, L.A., Adama, Mr. Bangura, Ya Mary Lane, Saidu, Isotu. Sainy. The girl with the white crayon. Marie.

There is much to be done. You know that.

I learned in Kamakwie that it is not anger that will fix injustice.

It is love. Boundless.

For information on how you can help, please visit kamakwie.org.

INTERVIEW WITH THE AUTHOR

Why did you decide to go to Sierra Leone?

One day, a woman I did not know named Karen Reedman phoned me to ask if I would write a book about child poverty in Sierra Leone. She worked at that time for World Hope Canada, which had received a Public Engagement Fund grant from the Canadian International Development Agency (CIDA) that could help support such a book.

Karen had asked Jane Buss, then executive director of the Writers' Federation of Nova Scotia, whom she should call. Jane, typical of her many kindnesses to me, gave her my number.

Neither of them knew that on the wall behind my desk was an ad for international aid that I had torn from a magazine years earlier. The top of the ad shows a blue sky with a scattering of clouds. The bottom is a black-and-white photograph of two little girls standing in patterned dresses on a patch of dirt. Each of the girls balances a gun in her hands, little fingers pressed tightly against its weight.

As Karen discussed the project with me, I turned to look at that ad, thinking that I couldn't remember what there was about it that had called me to put it up. I wondered, then, how I could say anything but "yes" to Karen.

You are particularly intent on readers seeing the individuals clearly. Do you think people from the West tend to look at the people of African countries as a single mass?

The people I met in Sierra Leone — the people in countries all over the developing world — need help from the rest of us. They need our money and our time and all of the skills we can offer them. But it is hard to be moved to act by people whose stories you don't know. I remember being on the ferry from the airport to Freetown. Heather and Janet were talking to

Brimah Samura about the people they knew in Kamakwie — catching up on the news. And I listened, but I had no frame of reference for what they were talking about. I didn't know the people. I couldn't imagine the personalities. I couldn't connect with what they were saying. My focus in this book on telling people's individual stories is an attempt to balance that — to help readers know and care about the people I was lucky enough to meet in person. Then, maybe the next time they see an image of someone suffering, they'll be able to respond in a different way. They may remember White Boy or Sainy or Marie.

Did you experience culture shock during your visit to Kamakwie?

I was lucky that this was my second trip to the developing world. My first trip was to visit the Darjeeling region of India, where my mum's cousin Fr. Abraham has lived and worked to alleviate poverty for more than sixty years. My parents had been closely involved with his multitude of projects since I was a child, so it was a "safe" introduction to the reality of poverty for me. Nonetheless, I was shattered by what I saw. There was nothing in my life's experience that could adequately prepare me for what starvation looked like. Not just the physical reality of children dressed in rags, their bodies wracked with hunger, but also the crushing injustice of it. But then in India — as in Sierra Leone — there was an unaccountable joy. Amidst squalor there was singing and laughing and dancing and an abundance of love. And there was nothing in my life's experience that could adequately prepare me for that, either.

So when I got to Sierra Leone, I was ready for those things, and I'm glad of that. It allowed me to concentrate in a different way. But what I was not prepared for was what I learned about war there. I took courses in peace and conflict as an undergrad at the University of Toronto, so I thought I approached the subject with some level of understanding. But no. The reality — the depth of the horror and its aftermath — was an incredible shock to me — and especially so because I cared about the people it affected.

What seemed most familiar to you as you met the people?

I've been lucky to travel to a lot of places around the world. And what I found in Sierra Leone is the same as what I've found in other countries. Humans are remarkably similar. We are funny and intelligent and generous and loving and creative — and frustrating and stubborn — just in different languages.

It seems that you have left a part of yourself in Kamakwie. Have you had thoughts about returning there — and, if so, how would a second visit be different from the first?

When I went to Kamakwie, I assumed it would be my only trip there. I had no intention of returning. And then every time we ran into Reverend Alusine — who was usually teasing and laughing — he'd become very serious and say, "We will pray that you will return to Kamakwie." At first it made me uneasy — people praying for me to come back. It felt like so much pressure. And I wasn't sure what I could do that would be useful after this book was written. Heather and Janet and Nathan and Jenn had such obvious talents. I have never had the remotest interest in medicine — and I lamented that in Sierra Leone. But then I started to really think about what Reverend Alusine said. It wasn't, "I will pray that more doctors come." It was that "you will return." He knew that it takes all kinds of skills to help. So I started to think about what I could do — what might make sense given my background. I would love to build a library in Kamakwie. When I do go back, I'll be working on that.

Your story of Kamakwie and the people you met there is moving and eloquent. If readers want some way of focusing their new-found concern for the children and others in that community, what suggestions or advice would you give them about making a contribution?

The best place to find this information is on the book's Web site: kamakwie.org.

ACKNOWLEDGMENTS

I am incredibly grateful to Karen Reedman, Jane Buss, World Hope Canada, and the Canadian International Development Agency (CIDA)'s Public Engagement Fund, collectively responsible for sending me to Sierra Leone to begin this book. That journey cracked open my world in important ways. I saw and heard things that haunt me. I saw and heard things that sent my soul soaring — that etched a new layer of beauty across my understanding of humanity.

I am so glad to have shared my time in Sierra Leone with Jennifer Becker, Heather Logan, Janet Roth, and Nathan Wickett. Their knowledge, concern, and humor never failed to ease the challenges implicit in the work I was doing.

I am most grateful to the people in Sierra Leone who allowed me to formally interview them. They are: Alusine Bangura, Brickson (Brimah) Bangura, Edward L. Bangura, John A. Bangura, Kadiatu Bangura, Binty Conteh, L.A. Contch, Dora Dumbuya, Sainy Alimamy Dumbuya, Soko Dumbuya, Stanley Dumbuya, Steven Lansana Kamara, Abu Bakar Kamora, Saidu Kanu, Marie Kargbo, Santigia Kargbo, Adama Koroma, Fatmata Irish Koroma, Mariama (Maria) Koroma, Sallay Mansaray, Brimah Samura, Umaro Samura, Medlym Kombiabai Sesay, Saidu Sesay, Alimamy Turay, Anthony Jacob Turay, Joseph (J.B.T.) Turay, and Musu Turay. I am equally grateful to the many adults and children I spent time with who helped me better understand life in Kamakwie. I wish I could have included each of them in the text of this book.

My friend Rugi Jalloh is my Canadian link to Sierra Leone, and has patiently answered my questions. Her easy laugh and open heart are constant reminders for me of the people I met in her home country. My Nova Scotian friend Joanne Taylor lived in Sierra Leone for a few years when she was a young woman. Her enduring love for that country and her enthusiasm about this book helped me begin. Naomi Wolf of the Woodhull Institute for Ethical Leadership gave me the insight I needed to proceed. My friend Tim Clarke, with characteristic generosity and skill, helped me fine-tune the photographs in this book.

Dr. Shelly Whitman of Dalhousie University made it possible for me to speak with Lieutenant-General Roméo Dallaire about this book and to participate in an early meeting of the Child Soldiers Initiative (CSI) that included Ishmael Beah and his colleagues from the Network of Young People Affected by War. The impact on me of both of those events reverberates still. I am also grateful to Tanya Zayed at CSI, and hope that this book will be useful in CSI's work to eradicate the use of child soldiers in the world (childsoldiersinitiative.org).

My mum's cousin Fr. J. Murray Abraham, S.J., has spent more than sixty years working to end poverty in the Darjeeling District of India. He is wise beyond telling and in this project, as throughout my life, I have been the beneficiary of both his knowledge and his love.

I have young children, and sometimes finding the time and quiet necessary to write required finding family and friends to help my husband, Mike James, and I care for them. In this we owe particular thanks to Hannah, Lara and Maddie Baldwin, Mary Jane Hatton, Jane James, Joe James, Heather Matthews, and Meghan McCharles.

I am grateful to Cheryl Chen, Pooja Tripathi and Michael Wallace at Red Deer Press, and also to Richard Dionne, its publisher. Richard was generous with his time and attention. His interest in this book at all stages of its development exemplifies the care and respect that are hallmarks of Red Deer.

That you picked up this book at all is a tribute to the talents of Blair Kerrigan, who designed it. His work was a singular act of imagination; making visual sense of the relationship between the words and photographs in this book required enormous skill. I am indebted to him for helping me tell this story.

Peter Carver edited this book. But first he waited for it — for more than a year. If he found that frustrating, I never knew it. With me he was endlessly patient and trusting, and I am truly grateful for that. Peter is a gifted editor, and I am lucky to have worked with him. This book is immeasurably better for his contributions. He is also smart, kind, and funny, and I'm grateful for those things, too.

I would not have written this book without my friend Laurie McNeill. She cheered, she cajoled, she listened, she encouraged, she read, she advised, and she loved — both me and what I was trying to do.

Jim Martin is the nicest big brother anyone could hope for, so I knew I would have his unfailing support in this project as in everything. But he also proved to be a sensitive, thoughtful reader. It was he who wanted to know more about Steven.

There is a lot of my dad, James Martin, in this book, though he died not long after I returned from Sierra Leone. Some of our last conversations were about this project. My dad had a deep understanding of the injustice of poverty and an abiding sense of our responsibility to help eliminate it; he had a hatred of war and a craving for peace that infused even the smallest aspects of our lives. The strength of that is here, as are, I hope, echoes of his intelligence, reason, and warmth.

My mum, Kathy Martin, had a role in this project that is hard to define, stretching as it does back to the beginnings of me. As I worked on this book, my mum read and listened and gave me lots of ideas. But it was more than just that. The courage with which she traveled alone across the world — for the first time without my dad — to help ease the poverty of the people in and near Kurseong, India, also mattered. She will understand when I say that this story, born of SASAC, is the most complete thanks I can offer her.

Mike and our children, Aidan, Kate, and Kieran, each sacrificed something important to allow me the chance to travel, to think, to write. I know the depth of what they gave and the grace with which they gave it. Their love for me and for the people I met in Sierra Leone doesn't know how to stop.